ARABIC LANGUAGE HANDBOOK

ARABIC LANGUAGE HANDBOOK

Mary Catherine Bateson

Georgetown University Press
Washington, D.C.

Georgetown University Press, Washington, D.C.

Printed in the United States of America

10 9 8 7 6 5 4 3 2 1 2003

This book is printed on acid-free recycled paper meeting the requirements of the American National Standard for Permanence in Paper for Printed Library Materials.

The map on p. xiv is reprinted with the permission of the Intercultural Press, Inc. from the International Press, Inc. from *Understanding Arabs: A Guide for Westerners,* by Margaret K. Nydell, 1996, p. ix.

Library of Congress Cataloging-in-Publication Data

Bateson, Mary Catherine.
Arabic language handbook / Mary Catherine Bateson.
p. cm.—(Georgetown classics in Arabic language and linguistics)
Originally published [Washington] : Center for Applied Linguistics, 1967.
Includes bibliographical references (p.).
ISBN 0-87840-386-8 (pbk. : alk. paper)
1. Arabic language. I. Title. II. Series.

PJ6095 .B3 2003
592.7'8242–dc21 2002033904

GEORGETOWN CLASSICS IN ARABIC LANGUAGE AND INGUISTICS

Karin C. Ryding and Margaret Nydell, series editors

For some time, Georgetown University Press has been interested in making available seminal publications in Arabic language and linguistics that have gone out of print. Some of the most meticulous and creative scholarship of the last century was devoted to the analysis of Arabic language and to producing detailed reference works and textbooks of the highest quality. Although some of the material is dated in terms of theoretical approaches, the content and methodology of the books considered for the reprint series is still valid and in some cases unsurpassed.

With global awareness now refocused on the Arab world, and with renewed interest in Arab culture, society, and political life, it is essential to provide easy access to classic reference materials such as dictionaries and reference grammars, and language teaching materials. The key components of this series of classic reprints have been chosen for quality of research and scholarship, and have been updated with new bibliographies and an introduction to provide readers with resources for further study.

Georgetown University Press hopes hereby to serve the growing national and international need for reference works on Arabic language and culture, as well as provide access to quality textbooks and audiovisual resources for teaching Arabic language in its written and spoken forms.

Books in the Georgetown Classics in Arabic Language and Linguistic series:

Arabic Language Handbook
Mary Catherine Bateson

A Basic Course in Moroccan Arabic
Richard S. Harrell with Mohammed Abu-Talib and William S. Carroll

TABLE OF CONTENTS

FOREWORD

As a concise outline of the Arabic language, Mary Catherine Bateson's *Arabic Language Handbook* has no peer. It was originally published in 1967 by the Center for Applied Linguistics as part of a series of handbooks for the languages of Africa and Asia, and nothing quite like it has appeared since, although research in Arabic linguistics has expanded dramatically over the past forty years (see, for example, the online bibliography of the Arabic Linguistic Society at www.umich.edu/~archive/linguistics/texts/biblio/arablingbib.txt.

Most scholarly publications in Arabic linguistics focus on particular features of the language (e.g., morphology, syntax, phonology, discourse analysis, dialectology, diglossia). A few books have recently been published that cover a wide range of topics in Arabic, for example: Clive Holes' *Modern Arabic* (Longman, 1995) and Kees Versteegh's *The Arabic Language* (Columbia University Press, 1997). However, Bateson's handbook is still the most streamlined reference for researchers, linguists, students, area specialists, and others interested in Arabic. As interest in the Arabic language increases, there is a pressing need for a solid, introductory handbook, and Georgetown University Press, working with the Georgetown University Department of Arabic Language, Literature, and Linguistics, is therefore reprinting this useful resource.

I used this book for my first course in Arabic linguistics, with Wallace Erwin in 1970, and I find that students still appreciate the book's conciseness, its thoroughness, and the clear writing style of Dr. Bateson. As a source for fundamental understanding of Arabic structures and of issues in Arabic linguistics from dialectology to literature, it is still a treasure. Although sections of the text need to be updated, the core information on the structure of the language remains accurate within the paradigm of structural linguistics. We are grateful to Dr. Bateson and the Center for Applied Linguistics for their permission to reprint.

Updates are provided in the preface and the bibliography. The accompanying map of Arabic-speaking countries has also been revised. In her preface, written in 1964, Bateson states that Arabic has 80 million speakers in "more than a dozen" states. Current figures show that the number of Arabic speakers has increased to almost 200 million in 20 states. The original bibliography has been expanded by Professors Margaret Nydell (dialectology) and Karin Ryding (linguistics and literature).

Karin C. Ryding
Georgetown University

PREFACE

THIS HANDBOOK is designed to give the kind of information about Arabic which will be useful to a student of the language, a specialist in the region where Arabic is spoken, or a linguist interested in learning about the structure and use of one of the world's principal languages. Part of the handbook (Chapter 1) is devoted to explaining what Arabic is like. All the important features of the grammar are discussed, but they are arranged to demonstrate how the language functions rather than to teach students how to manipulate it. The remainder of the book is devoted to describing the use of Arabic: how it has been used for speech and writing since our earliest records of it and how it is used today in the modern Arab world where new governmental structures and technologies are being adapted.

Modern Arabic has eighty million speakers and is the language of more than a dozen states. Historically, Arabic has been one of the great languages of civilization, accompanying Islam across North Africa and down the coast of East Africa, up into Central Asia and across Southeast Asia as a liturgical language, preserving Greek science through the Middle Ages, and developing a rich literary tradition with which Europe is mainly familiar in one of its popular forms, the *Arabian Nights.* Formally, Arabic is totally unrelated to English and is the most important member of the Semitic group of languages with an intricate and unfamiliar structure.

The use of Arabic is involved with a special social situation which must be understood in order to deal with the area: the Classical language, which was the vehicle of Islam and of the literature and is the primary written form today, is relatively uniform throughout the Arab world and across the Islamic centuries, but has never been the ordinary spoken language of the Arabs. Colloquial Arabic is the language of normal conversation, but it varies in ways which reflect all the geographical, social, and religious heterogeneity of the population. This situation is called *diglossia* and presents problems both for description and for the Arabs themselves. Chapter 2 describes the development of Classical Arabic up to the modern period and Chapter 3 describes modern developments in Classical Arabic, its present use in relation to the colloquial dialects, and the origins and structures of the dialects.

Since this is a handbook and not a scholarly volume, references have been kept to a minimum. A bibliography has been included at the end which contains works in English which would be useful as further reading on the topics dealt with here. Many of the items in the bibliography, such as Wright's *Grammar* and Nicholson's *History of Arabic Literature,* have been extremely useful in preparing this handbook but are not generally acknowledged. Notes have been inserted in the text only for highly specific material or examples taken from sources which are not mentioned in the general bibliography. On the other hand, the bibliography itself has been designed to include references to books with longer and more specialized bibliographies for more advanced work.

M.C.B.
Harvard University
December 1964

NOTATIONS

All linguistic citations of Arabic material are given in a phonemic transcription (see 1.2). Roots are italicized; all other material is enclosed within slant lines. Where attention is directed to some phonetic detail the material is enclosed within square brackets. For Arabic words and phrases that are not cited as linguistic examples a more conventional transcription is used.

SYMBOLS AND ABBREVIATIONS:

/ /	encloses phonemic transcription
[ ]	encloses phonetic transcription
' '	encloses glosses or translations
-	indicates a point of affixation
°	indicates division of a linguistic form at the end of a line
*	indicates a hypothetical or reconstructed form
>	'developed to, became' (historical change)
<	'developed from' (historical change)
→	'appears as, becomes' (grammatical process)
←	'results from' (grammatical process)
~	'alternates with; or'
C	a consonant
v	a vowel
$\bar{v}$	a long vowel
$\underset{\wedge}{V}$	a semivowel (w or y)
C_1, C_2...	identifies position of C in a root or word
ClA	Classical Arabic
CoA	Colloquial Arabic

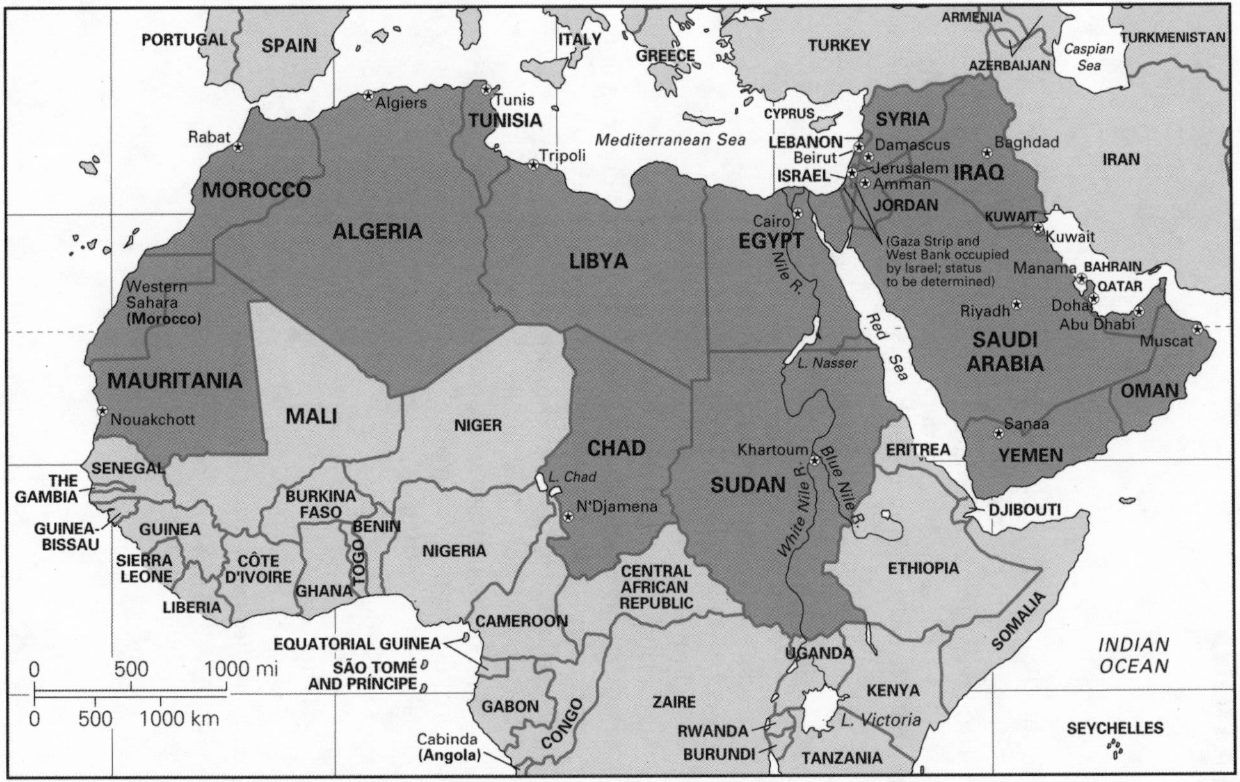

Map of Arabic-Speaking Countries of Nothern Africa and the Middle East

1. AN OUTLINE OF ARABIC STRUCTURE

1.1 General features

Before launching into a systematic sketch of the linguistic structure of Classical Arabic, it seems worthwhile to provide a general outline of the derivational processes which characterize Arabic, and which are more highly developed in Arabic than in other Semitic languages.

Arabic operates by what is known as the 'root and pattern system', which is the hallmark of the Semitic languages and their most striking feature. Roots usually consist of three consonants, e.g. *klm*. These consonant sequences, unpronounceable in themselves, have one or sometimes several general meanings: the root *klm* means something to do with speech. Roots cannot be used, however, unless they are provided with vowels, and may be specifically defined only when in association with a particular vowel pattern, e.g. /kalimah/ 'word, utterance, maxim', utilizing the pattern $C_1aC_2iC_3ah$, where $C_1C_2C_3$ represent the three consonants of the root in relation to the surrounding vowels. Some patterns require the lengthening (gemination) of one of the root consonants: /kallam/ 'he addressed (someone)' has the pattern $C_1aC_2C_2aC_3$. Some patterns involve the affixation of additional consonants: /kalmānīy/ 'eloquent, fluent speaker', from the pattern $C_1aC_2C_3$ānīy, or /mutakallim/ 'spokes-man, theologian', from the pattern muta$C_1aC_2C_2iC_3$. These patterns, while not perfectly systematic, do in many cases have clearly definable functions, and the attempt to define these functions makes up a great part of the grammatical study of Arabic, whereas the listing of roots is essentially the business of the dictionary. If this aspect of Arabic structure were perfectly systematic, the lexicographer would only need to list the roots, and the speaker could combine them at will with the desired pattern to express, e.g. 'the place where such and such takes place', 'a professional practitioner of such and such', 'one who pretends to be such and such', etc. Unfortunately, this is not the case, and the exploration of an Arabic dictionary is a disillusioning business.

The dictionary is arranged by roots according to the order of the consonantal alphabet, but must spell out in each case what semantic content does in fact result from the combination of a particular root and a particular pattern. The bewildering meanings given in the dictionary for forms that ought to have been predictable may be assigned to several causes: (a) the association of the root with more than one area of meaning: the root *klm* has a number of forms which refer to wounds and wounding; (b) a cultural and historical understanding of a particular concept which may escape the Western student: the meaning 'theologian' for /mutakallim/ would probably fit in this category; in such cases the meanings seem unrelated and arbitrary in English but are at least to some degree systematic; (c) a series of historical accidents which must be explored for each word: for instance, the use of a particular word which ought to mean either 'maternal' or 'popular, pertaining to the people or nation', for the meaning 'illiterate', may be traced to the readiness of the Muslim theologians to accept a farfetched derivation in order to find a verse of the Qur'ān which proved that Muhammad had not known how to read. However, it is probably more accurate to think of the specificity of particular patterns as a graduated characteristic which has increased slowly by the application of analogy, so that the root and pattern system may be more symmetrical in Arabic than it was in Proto-Semitic.

In dealing with the root and pattern system, it may be helpful to consider that: (a) most patterns, even in what are called pausal forms (see 1.24), provide some information about the place of a particular form in the system of parts of speech, e.g. as a verb form or a noun form; (b) many patterns are the result of a series of derivational steps, some of which are semantically systematic, while others seem arbitrary: the meanings of derived forms of the verb are often startling, though the participles derived from those verb forms stand in a predictable relationship to them; (c) some forms are almost totally predictable, and, if the form does not already exist, will be given a predictable meaning when coined, up to the point where some historical accident intervenes. Accordingly, the discussion of derivation (see 1.3) will be, to some extent, an idealized one, presenting generalizations which may not hold up in practice.

1.2 Phonology

1.21 *Consonants*

The Arabic writing system is in many ways a fair reflection of the linguistic facts of the language. It contains 28 signs, each of which represents a consonant which may act as one of the three consonants of a root. Since there is some variation in the pronunciation of the consonants in different parts of the Arabic-speaking world, even in formal reading, transcriptions have been chosen which seem to reflect the internal structure of the phonological system (see Table 1). The so-called 'emphatics' of Arabic, which tend to produce a lowering of the vowels in their immediate vicinity, are grouped together in the center column, along with other consonants which may have a similar effect, even though there is no other set of consonants formed in that part of the mouth which do not affect the vowels.

Such a scheme must be qualified in a number of ways.

The emphatics, which are generally velarized, or articulated farther to the back of the mouth than the non-emphatics, vary considerably, even in their formal pronunciation. They were probably all voiced at one time:

Modern pronunciation:	**Early Arabic voiced emphatics:**
ض /ḍ/	[ẓ$^{\lambda}$] lateralized dental fricative
ط /ṭ/	[ḍ] dental stop
ظ /ẓ/	[ḏ] interdental fricative
ص /ṣ/	[ẓ] dental spirant

Thus in Early Arabic there was a voiced emphatic corresponding to each voiced-voiceless pair of dentals and interdentals. A similar relationship may once have existed between /j/, /k/, and /q/: /j/, which is pronounced as either [ž] or [dž], corresponds

Table 1

The Consonants of Classical Arabic

	PLAIN CONSONANTS		EMPHATIC AND EMPHATIC-LIKE CONSONANTS		SONANTS	
	voiced	*unvoiced*	*voiced*	*unvoiced*		
Labial	b ب	f ف			m م	w و
Interdental	*d* ز	*t* ث				
Dental	d ر	t ت	ḍ ض	ṭ ط		
	z ز	s ʔ	ẓ ظ	ṣ ص		
					n ن	
Lateral			(ḷ)		l ل	
Trill					r ر	
Palatal	j ج	š ش				y ي
		k ك				
Velar			ġ غ	x خ		
Uvular				q ق		
Pharyngeal			ε ع	ḥ ح		
Glottal		ʔ ء				
		h ه				

to the [g] of other Semitic languages; /q/ was originally voiced, and is still so in all modern Bedouin dialects. Some remnants of the earlier pronunciation of the emphatics may be found in Arabian dialects and in the related Semitic languages grouped as South Arabic (see 2.1).

The emphatic [ḷ] does not appear as a letter of the alphabet, but it seems clear that it must be given the theoretical status of a separate phoneme, although it is easier in dealing with Classical Arabic to specify the contexts in which it occurs, i.e. in some contexts in the name of God.[1]

It is worth noting some of the limitations on the occurrence of the consonants. Only a small number of them—/m w t s n y ʾ/—may appear as derivational and inflectional affixes, along with / l h *d* k/, which are used quite extensively in different derivational processes in the system of particles. The emphatics and the less familiar back consonants are almost completely limited to the lexicon of triliteral roots. All of the consonants may be doubled, but there are limitations, in some morphological contexts, on the appearance of the same consonant twice with only a short vowel intervening: -C_2vC_3, when C_2 = C_3, tends to become -(v)C_2C_3, if the remaining structure allows. Regardless of root affiliation, initial *ʾvʾ- → /ʾv̄- /, and there are sporadic cases described in the classical grammars of the reduction of /tata-/ to /ta-/, etc. In the formation of roots, C_2 = C_3 is common, but C_1 and C_2 are never identical.

In Proto-Semitic, verbal roots appear not to have been formed from consonants produced in the same region of the mouth. Although there has been some shift in articulation, this still means that members of the following classes tend not to occur side by side: the back consonants and the palatals (except /š/ and /y/); the dental and interdental stops and fricatives (with /š/); the liquids; and the labials /f b m/ (but not /w/)[2].

1.22 *Vowels*

The newcomer to Arabic is often aware of a great variation in the vowels, most of which is automatically produced by the consonantal environment. The basic vowel system consists of three vowels /a i u/ with their corresponding long forms /ā ī ū/, although some ancient forms of Arabic seem to have had a fourth long vowel /ē/ in some positions of modern /ā/, whose occurrence is referred to as *imāla* 'inclination [of the ā toward the ī]'. There is some controversy over the most illuminating analysis of the long vowels and of the diphthongs /aw/ and /ay/. The Arabic orthography treats the long vowels /ī/ and /ū/ as combinations of a short vowel (supplied by the reader) and a semivowel, i.e. as diphthongs /iy/ and /uw/, analogous to /ay/

and /aw/—while for long /ā/, the orthographic sign called *alif* is used to represent the lengthening element. This procedure has a partial grammatical justification in that /y/ and /w/ often enter into the word as root consonants and act phonetically as the second element of a diphthong whose first element is /a/, or of a long vowel to which a preceding /i/ or /u/ assimilates: iy, uy → /ī/; uw, iw → /ū/; but this is balanced by the many cases in which no defensible notation will indicate the process by which a semivowel has been absorbed: awa → /ā/. In the present analysis, the symbolizations /ā ī ū ay aw/ have been used, but morphological processes may sometimes result in /iy/ or /uw/, which must then be considered identical with /ī/ and /ū/.

The strict limitations on the environments within which grammatical /y/ and /w/ can retain their phonological value and the ramifications of their behavior produce the system of 'weak' nouns and verbs which causes such difficulty to the student. /w/ may be followed by any vowel at the beginning of a word, while initial /y/ cannot precede /i/. Either, if preceded by the corresponding short vowel or short /a/, may be followed only by a consonant, a long vowel, or a short /a/; and if the /y/ or /w/ is a consonant of the root it is generally eliminated between two short /a/'s. After a consonant, the sequence semivowel + vowel generally yields a long vowel, and after /ā/, a single semivowel often becomes /ʾ/. When impossible sequences would occur, such as *iwu or *ūyi, they are resolved in a number of different ways, depending on the morphological context.

1.23 *Syllable structure*

Arabic is a language in which meaningful contrasts depend on both vowel and consonant length. Two basic syllable types are permitted, with a third, aberrant type in special cases.

All Arabic syllables must begin with a single consonant; the simplest type is Cv, a consonant plus a short vowel, e.g. /huwa/ 'he', /šariba/ 'he drank', with two and three short syllables respectively. A long syllable either contains a long vowel, Cv̄, or has the form CvC where another syllable with its own initial consonant follows. For example, /qablī/ 'before me' has a first syllable of the type CvC (qab) and a second syllable Cv̄ (-lī), but since, as has been pointed out above, /lī/ could be written /liy/, these two ways of forming long syllables in Arabic are essentially equivalent. Syllables of the type Cv̄C are termed overlong and rarely occur.

On the whole, syllable formation is very regular in Arabic, though the handling of weak roots (containing /y/ or /w/) is complicated by the fact that after their forms have been simplified to remove impossible vowel sequences, their syllabic structure must also be brought in line, e.g. *mašay- + -at → *mašayat → *mašāt → /mašat/ 'she walked'.

Under certain conditions, a cluster of consonants may be grammatically formed at the beginning of a word (if the word has the definite article, or is an imperative of the first form of the verb, or is an imperative, a perfect, or a verbal noun of some of the derived verbs). If such a word is preceded by a word ending in an open syllable, the two words are run together in pronunciation: /fawqa/ 'above' + /lbayt/ 'the house' → /fawqalbayt/. Such examples are normally written as separate words in the Arabic orthography. If the word is preceded by a word ending in a consonant—there are relatively few cases in which this can happen—an anaptyctic vowel is supplied: /a/ if the first word is /min/ 'from': /mina lbayt/ 'from the house'; /u/ if the last syllable of the first word is a pronominal suffix ending in /-um/: /wajadtumu lbayt/ 'you (masc. pl.) found the house': and /i/ in all other cases: /wajadati lbayt/ 'she found the house'. If the consonant cluster appears after silence, both an anaptyctic vowel and a consonant (always a glottal stop) must be supplied, i.e. *CCv → *vCCv → ˀvCCv. This anaptyctic vowel is always /a/ for the definite article: /ˀalbayt/ 'the house'; and /i/ for verbal forms and elsewhere, unless the vowel following the cluster is /u/, in which case it is also /u/; the anaptyctic vowel is not indicated in isolated citations in this study. When loans from other languages are assimilated into Arabic, they are altered to fit this pattern: /ˀiqlīm/ 'climate', /faransā/ 'France'.

1.24 *Stress and pausal forms*

Classical Arabic has two further phonological features which deserve mention, although the one is automatic and the other stylistic and thus do not play the role of distinguishing meanings.

Stress in ClA is automatically produced by the syllable structure of the word: the stress falls either on the long syllable nearest to the end of the word (except for the final syllable), or on the first syllable: /kátaba/ 'he wrote', /katábta/ 'you (masc. sing.) wrote,' /takā́taba/ 'the two (masc.) corresponded.' A major deviation from this rule occurs in many pronunciations of ClA, where, in words with an initial long syllable followed by three short ones, the stress may not be more than three syllables from the end of the word: /maktabatun/ 'library' may be stressed on either the first or the second syllable. Changes in syllable structure in the dialects have produced instances, although not a great many, in which stress distinguishes meaning.

The standard style of reading ClA includes a set of conventions for dropping final short vowels and dropping or shortening the case endings at the end of phrases or in isolation where words appear in 'pause form'. These conventions appear to be part of the rhyme structure of even very early poetry, and since the system of case inflection constitutes one of the main differences between ClA and all the colloquials, many speakers of Arabic extend the use of pause forms as much as possible in their use of Classical.

In the pause forms, which will generally be used for citations in this study when case or modal endings are not in question, all words are stripped of the final /-n/ which follows the case ending on indefinite nouns and the case ending itself or any final short vowel, and the feminine ending is reduced from /-at-/ to /-ah/ (often pronounced /-a/). The exception to this rule is the final /-an/ of the indefinite accusative, which becomes /-ā/ or, in less formal usage, is retained, as it will be in all citations here. Examples of context forms: /maktabatun/ 'library' (indef. nom.): /baytan/ 'house' (indef. accus.): /lmutakallimu/ 'the theologian' (def. nom.): these same forms would be realized in pause as /maktabah/, /baytā/ ~ /baytan/, and /lmutakallim/ (/ʾalmutakallim/, with the initial cluster resolved).

1.3 The noun

The Arab grammarians have traditionally dealt with Arabic in terms of only three classes of words: nouns, verbs, and particles. This analysis will be retained here, except that the pronouns will be included with the particles, roughly defined as the class of words (except unassimilated loanwords) which resist efforts at analysis in terms of the root and pattern system. Adjectives are not formally distinct from nouns, and there is no separate class of adverbs.

For both nouns and verbs, a discussion of the inflectional system, which operates primarily but not exclusively by affixation, will precede a discussion of the derivational systems, which involve the total rearrangement of the vowels in their relations to the root consonants—the imposition of new patterns. While there is some similarity between the two inflectional systems—each expresses some of the same obligatory categories in slightly varying ways—a more tangled path must be followed to deal with the derivational systems: nouns derived from simple verbs are included in the initial discussion of noun derivation, whereas nouns derived from derived verbs are discussed in relation to the verbs themselves.

1.31 *Noun inflection*

Arabic nouns are inflected for case, determination, gender (masculine and feminine), and number (singular, collective, dual, plural).

1.311 *Case and determination*

The role played by Arabic nouns in the sentence is usually indicated by short vowel suffixes: there are three cases, traditionally referred to as the nominative, genitive, and accusative, but their functions are not precisely those we generally associate with these terms. For the majority of indefinite Arabic nouns, these short vowels are followed by a final /-n/, not indicated on the cursive line, called 'nunation'. The definite article is the commonest way of determining a noun; this is /l-/ prefixed to the noun and assimilated to any initial apical consonant: / *t d* t d s z ṭ ḍ ṣ ẓ n l r š/. These are called by the Arab grammarians 'sun letters', all other consonants being 'moon letters': /l-/ + /šams/ → /ššams/ 'the sun', in contrast with /lqamr/ 'the moon'. This is a morphologically conditioned assimilation whose domain has, however, been expanded to include various other grammatical juxtapositions of /l/ and these consonants in some dialects.

Nouns also become definite when followed by a determining complement, which may be a noun in the genitive: /baytu lmaliki/ 'the king's house'; or a suffixed pronoun: /baytu-hu/ 'his house'. They do not then have nunation or the definite article.

Context forms:

	Definite: 'the house'	*Indefinite*: 'a house'
Nominative	/lbaytu/	/baytun/
Genitive	/lbayti/	/baytin/
Accusative	/lbayta/	/baytan/

All nouns (except duals and 'sound plurals') follow this regular declension in the definite, but some distinctions may be lost because the final short vowel of the word base is followed by C_3 = /y/ or /w/ which has been changed into /y/ in the process of derivation, as frequently occurs.

If the vowel before the /y/ is /u/ or /i/, the theoretical forms are simplified as follows (root *qḍy*):

	Definite: 'the judge'	*Indefinite*: 'a judge'
Nominative	*lqāḍiyu → /lqāḍī/	*qāḍiyun → /qāḍin/
Genitive	*lqāḍiyi → /lqāḍī/	*qāḍiyin → /qāḍin/
Accusative	/lqāḍiya/	/qāḍiyan/

(Note that all active participles of weak-C_3 verbs and their verbal nouns in Forms V and VI follow this pattern.)

If the vowel before the /y/ is /a/, the simplification is even more drastic. From the root *hdy* we get the theoretical forms:

*lhudayu, *lhudayi, *lhudaya → /lhudā/ 'the (right) guidance', and the indefinite is, for all cases, /hudan/ '(right) guidance'. (Note that all passive participles of derived weak-C_3 verbs, as well as the commonest nouns of time and place derived from such roots, follow this pattern.)

Arabic also has a narrowly defined group of nouns which differ from the above in that in the indefinite they do not take nunation and in the genitive take short /a/, making the genitive identical with the accusative. These words, traditionally called diptotes, include: many proper nouns, including those of foreign origin; plurals with the pattern $C_1aC_2\bar{a}C_3i/\bar{i}C_4$; plurals and other grammatically feminine nouns ending with /-āʾ/ where the glottal stop does not represent a root consonant; comparatives and superlatives; and some other adjective types, as well as a number of minor classes and special cases. The indefinite declined forms of all these are subject to the same simplifications in the case of weak roots; the only surprising feature is the nunation of the nominative/genitive of diptotes with the same weakness as /qāḍī/ (see above), e.g. the theoretical form *mawāšiy- has /mawāšin/ for the nominative and genitive, with the expected /mawāšiya/ 'cattle' in the accusative. All totally indeclinable nouns are treated as are the diptotes ending in /-ay-/, i.e. they show no case distinctions at all: /rādiyū/ 'radio'.

Dual suffixes and the 'sound' plural suffixes, which may be used with a limited number of nouns (see below), do not differentiate the genitive and accusative: the so-called 'sound feminine plural' /-āt-/ takes nunation: nom. /lmalikātu/ 'the queens', /malikātun/ 'queens'; gen.-accus. /lmalikāti/, /malikātin/. The dual ending and the 'sound masculine plural' have endings which, especially for the masculine, are reminiscent of singular case endings, although lengthened. From the word /muslim/ 'Muslim, one who submits', we get for the plural: nom. /muslimūna/ 'Muslims'; gen.-accus. /muslimīna/; and for the dual: nom. /muslimāni/ 'two Muslims', gen.-accus. /muslimayni/. The final /n/ + short vowel remains when the noun is determined by the definite article: /lmuslimūna/ 'the Muslims'; but drops when the noun is followed by a determining complement: /muslimū baġdād/ 'the Muslims of Baghdad'.

1.312 *Gender*

Gender and number are obligatory categories in both the verb and the noun systems of Arabic.

Grammatically feminine nouns are modified by feminine adjectives and act as the subject of feminine verbs. Many grammatically feminine nouns are feminine in form, and have the feminine ending /-at-/, which is followed by the case ending: /kalimatun/ 'a word' (nom. indef.); pause form: /kalimah/. Two other endings appear as the feminine of certain derived forms: /-āˀ-/: /ṣṣaḥrāˀu/ 'the desert'; and /-ā/: /ddunyā/ 'the world'; both are diptotes. A small number of formally feminine nouns are grammatically masculine: /xalīfah/ 'caliph'. Many nouns which are not formally feminine are so grammatically: certain paired parts of the body: /yad/ 'hand'; names of countries, cities, and winds; /ˀarḍ/ 'earth'; states of being which are explicitly female (but not all of these): /εāqir/ 'barren woman'; and, above all, *all plurals which do not refer to rational beings*.

The use of masculine and feminine plural forms for verbs and modifiers is limited to nouns referring to rational beings.

1.313 *Number*

Number lies midway between purely inflectional processes and an exploitation of the root and pattern system that verges on the derivational. All duals, indicating a pair or two or any object, are formed by a suffix, and there are suffixes for masculine and feminine plurals—the so-called 'sound' plurals (see 1.311 for their case endings). These suffixes have initial vowels, and follow the last root consonant of the noun, except for the dual suffix, which follows the feminine ending if it is present.

	Nom. context forms	Nom. pause forms
Dual masculine	-ā(ni)	/baytān/ 'two houses'
Dual feminine	-ā(ni)	/malikatān/ 'two queens'
Sound masc. plural	-ū(na)	/muslimūn/ 'Muslims'
Sound fem. plural	-āt(un)	/malikāt/ 'queens'

The sound masculine plural is used primarily with participles of derived forms of the verb and with adjectives ending in /-ī(y)/: /sūrīyūn/ 'Syrians'. The sound feminine plural is used for the feminines of both the above; for many but not all words with feminine endings in the singular, especially for those which have corresponding masculine forms: /malikah/ 'queen' pl. /malikāt/ (compare /malik/ 'king')—this is true whether the feminine ending has been added to indicate feminine gender or for some other derivational reason; for some masculine nouns: /ḥammām/ 'bath' pl. /ḥammāmāt/—including many foreign ones; and for some feminines which lack the feminine ending in the singular. For simple bases of the form $C_1vC_2C_3$(ah), if the short vowel is /u/ or /a/, it is often reproduced after C_2 in forming sound plurals: /ɛurs/ 'marriage' pl. /ɛurusāt/, /ˀarḍ/ 'earth' pl. /ˀaraḍūn/. This is obligatory only where v=/a/.

The vast majority of Arabic nouns have 'broken' plurals. In these, the root consonants of the noun are rearranged with new vowels, consonantal elements may be supplied, and feminine endings are lost. There are some thirty possible patterns for broken plurals. Only a few of them are predictable from the singular, and many are also used with other roots to form singular nouns. Some of the most common broken plurals for words with three consonants are the following:

ˀaC_1C_2āC_3	/maṯal/ 'siˀmile, likeness' pl. /ˀamṯāl//sūq/ 'market' pl. /ˀaswāq/
C_1uC_2ūC_3	/dars/ 'study, lesson' pl. /durūs//bayt/ 'house' pl. /buyūt/
C_1iC_2āC_3	/rajul/ 'man' pl. /rijāl/
C_1uC_2uC_3	/kitāb/ 'book' pl. /kutub/
ˀaC_1C_2uC_3	/nahr/ 'river' pl. /ˀanhur/
C_1uC_2C_3ān	/balad/ 'town, country' pl. /buldān/

The first and fifth of these belong to the group of plurals traditionally called 'plurals of paucity', referring to fewer than ten, but this distinction only holds when another plural is in use. Many nouns have several plurals, sometimes with different meanings: /bayt/ ‘house’ has a second meaning ‘verse’, with the plural /ˀabyāt/.

While there are recurrent relationships between the form and meaning of the singular and the form of the plural, these are not usually sufficient for prediction. However, many nouns with either a long vowel, or four consonants, or both, fall into a somewhat regular pattern, as follows:

Singular	*Plural*
Cv̄CvC(ah)	CawāCiC (non rational)
	/εāmil/ ‘factor’, pl. /εawāmil/
	CuCCāC (rational)
	/εāmil/ ‘laborer’, pl. /εummāl/
CvCv̄C(ah)	CaCāˀiC (non-rational)
	/qasīmah/ ‘coupon’, pl. /qasāˀim/
	CuCaCāˀ, ˀaCCiCāˀ (rational)
	/qasīm/ ‘partner’, pl. /qusamāˀ/, /ˀaqsimāˀ/
CvCCvC(ah)	CaCāCiC (non-rational)
	/maktab/ ‘office’, /maktabah/ ‘library’ pl. of both /makātib/
	CaCāCiC CaCāCiCah (rational)
	/qayṣar/ ‘caesar’, pl. /qayāṣir/, /qayāṣirah/
CvCCv̄C(ah)	CaCāCīC (non-rational)
	/maktūb/ ‘letter’, pl. (makātib/
	CaCāCīC, CaCāCiCah (rational)
	/tilmīḏ/ ‘pupil’, pl. /talāmīḏ/, /talāmiḏah/

Most of these forms can be described by the formula $C_1aC_2\bar{a}C_3i/\bar{i}C_4$(ah), all of whose variants are diptotes except those with the feminine ending, which are in general the plurals of nouns refering to rational beings. Many of the types of singulars listed above have other possible plurals, but only those that seem to belong to this cluster of forms have been listed. Note that the /ī/ appears to lengthen some plurals corresponding to the bulkier singulars. Where there are fewer than four consonants in the singular, an additional consonant is supplied in the plural: for nouns with a long vowel in the first syllable: C_2=/w/; for nouns with a long vowel in the second syllable: C_3=/ʔ/. The presence of a feminine ending on the singular of nouns referring to rational beings has very little effect on the choice of plural.

Plurals belonging to this group are also sometimes used for nouns with more than four consonants, in which case one is usually dropped: /ɛankabūt/ 'spider' pl. /ɛanākib/.

The broken plurals are closely related to a rather vaguely defined group of words from which they may have developed, the collectives, which act rather like such English words as 'rice' or 'fruit'. Many originally collective nouns may have been assimilated either to the singular or the plural. The collectives which survive usually have a singular 'noun of unity', formed by adding a feminine ending, as well as a true plural: /tuffāḥ/ 'apples (col.)' resembles many such nouns (especially ones referring to plants and animals) in having a form /tuffāḥah/ 'one, single apple' with the plural /tuffāḥāt/ 'a number of single apples'. Another type of collective is formed by adding the feminine to adjectives: /lmuslimah/ 'the Muslims (col.)'.

1.32 *Noun derivation*

Except for the broken plurals, most of the previous discussion concerns the inflection of already formed noun bases, such as /malik/ 'king'. Such bases are, however, the result of the interlocking of at least two elements (see 1.1); in this example, the root *mlk*, with the vaguely defined meaning of dominion, and the pattern $C_1aC_2iC_3$, whose meaning and function may or may not be definable. Because patterns vary in their specificity, it is most efficient to approach them first formally.

1.321 *Noun derivation by shifting vowel patterns*

It has been demonstrated[3] that below the pattern of specific meanings for specific patterns, the possible patterns of Arabic nouns may be analyzed in terms of a range from the briefest possible forms the phonology allows: $C_1vC_2C_3$, augmented to $C_1vC_2vC_3$, and further augmented by lengthening either vowels or consonants (C_2 or C_3), with a tendency towards having the second syllable at least as long as the first, and with a preference for doubling C_2 to lengthen the first syllable rather than lengthening the first vowel. The assignment of specific meanings to specific patterns, often by the operation of analogy over long periods, is complemented by the tendency to use the bulkier forms as more emphatic or expressive (note that plurals are, in most cases, bulkier than their singulars). Table 2 shows the range of singular noun forms produced only by changes in patterns without affixation. The figures after the forms indicate by the number of digits the number of steps of increased derivational complexity. Where one form has 'given rise' to several bulkier forms, these are identified such that CuCC ⟨3⟩ 'gives rise' to ⟨31⟩ and ⟨32⟩, while ⟨31⟩ has in turn 'produced' ⟨311⟩ and ⟨312⟩; and ⟨32⟩, similarly, has ⟨321⟩, ⟨322⟩, ⟨323⟩ and ⟨324⟩—four derived forms, some of which have developed even further.

Arabic nouns appear with all of these shapes, with increasing specificity as we examine the bulkier forms. Among the simpler forms (the left-hand column) appear many primitive nouns as well as many nouns whose use is directly related to the first (underived) form of the verb. The following forms (many with the feminine ending) are used as verbal nouns, referring simply to the action of the verb:

⟨1⟩	⟨11⟩	⟨111⟩	⟨2⟩		⟨211⟩	⟨3⟩		⟨311⟩
	⟨12⟩	⟨122⟩		⟨22⟩	⟨221⟩		⟨32⟩	⟨321⟩
								⟨323⟩

The feminines of ⟨1⟩ and ⟨2⟩ have specific meanings: CaCCah, the doing of the action once; CiCCah, the manner of doing it. The form CāCiC ⟨121⟩, e.g. /kātib/ 'writer, scribe, writing', is the normal, productive active participle of the first form verb, but a number of other forms designate agents, although these are not generally productive:

⟨1⟩	⟨11⟩	⟨112⟩	⟨2⟩	⟨3⟩	⟨31⟩	
	⟨12⟩	⟨121⟩			⟨32⟩	⟨321⟩
		⟨122⟩				
	⟨13⟩	⟨131⟩				

Of these, CaCīC ⟨122⟩ and CaCūC ⟨131⟩ are associated with continual or habitual action. The first is especially common,

Table 2
Range of Singular Noun Forms Produced by Changes in Patterns

CaCC ⟨1⟩	CaCaC ⟨11⟩	CāCaC ⟨111⟩	
		CaCāC ⟨112⟩	CaC$_2$C$_2$āC ⟨1121⟩
		CaC$_2$C$_2$aC ⟨113⟩	
		CaCaC$_2$C$_3$ ⟨114⟩	
	CaCiC ⟨12⟩	CāCiC ⟨121⟩	
		CaCīC ⟨122⟩	CiCCi¯C ⟨1221⟩
	CaCuC ⟨13⟩	CaCūC ⟨131⟩	CaCCūC ⟨1311⟩
			CāCūC ⟨1312⟩
		CaCuCC ⟨132⟩	
CiCC ⟨2⟩	CiCiC ⟨21⟩	CiCiCC ⟨211⟩	
	CiCaC ⟨22⟩	CiCāC ⟨221⟩	CiCCāC ⟨2211⟩
		CiCCaC ⟨222⟩	
		CiCaCC ⟨223⟩	
CuCC ⟨3⟩	CuCuC ⟨31⟩	CuCūC ⟨311⟩	
		CuCuCC ⟨312⟩	
	CuCaC ⟨32⟩	CuCāC ⟨321⟩	CuCCāC ⟨3221⟩
		CuCCaC ⟨322⟩	
		CuCaCC ⟨323⟩	
		CuCayC ⟨324⟩	CuCCayC ⟨3241⟩

producing large classes of familiar nouns: /ṭawīl/ 'long, tall (being long)', /ṣadīq/ 'friend (being true, reliable)'. Moving from these further to the right, we find a whole series of intensive forms: ⟨1121⟩ ⟨1311⟩ ⟨1312⟩ ⟨2211⟩ ⟨322⟩ ⟨3221⟩: /širrīb/ 'drunkard', /sabbūḥ/ 'all pure, all glorious', etc. CaCCāC ⟨1121⟩ has acquired, by analogy with Aramaic borrowings, the specific use of the name of a profession: /xayyāṭ/ 'tailor', /najjār/ 'carpenter'; the same form with the feminine ending added is used for the instrument of habitual activity: the /ṭayyār/ 'aviator' flies a /ṭayyārah/, whereas for the other intensives the feminine ending is more likely to denote increased intensity.

Among the columns on the right-hand side of the chart, the particular semantic content of a root gives to the simple idea of intensity a number of connotations: pejorative, diminutive, or augmentative. In addition, Arabic has a set form for the diminutive: CuCayC ⟨324⟩, e.g. /kalb/ 'dog' /kulayb/ 'little dog', which can be used quite freely. Other partially standardized uses of patterns are CiCāC ⟨221⟩ for a container or tool: /jirāb/ 'bag'; CuCāC ⟨321⟩ for a disease; /suεāl/ 'cough'; CiCāCah for a function or office; /wizārah/ 'ministry'. It is also worth noting the large number of these patterns (with a preference for the third group, containing /u/ in the first syllable) that are used for broken plurals or collectives:

⟨11⟩	⟨2⟩	⟨22⟩	⟨221⟩	⟨3⟩	⟨31⟩	⟨311⟩	
					⟨32⟩		⟨3212⟩
						⟨322⟩	

1.322 *Noun derivation by affixation*

A further group of Arabic noun patterns involves affixes containing the consonants /m t n y ˀ/. Many of these are specifically related to verbs; only those related to simple verbs will be discussed here, while nouns related to derived verbs will be discussed later.

(a) *Prefix* /m-/

(1) $maC_1C_2i/aC_3(ah)$ indicates either the time or the place of an action: /maktab/ 'office', /maktabah/ 'library', (/katab/ 'write'); /majlis/ 'session' (/jalas/ 'sit'); /mawεid/ 'time or place of rendezvous' (/waεad/ 'promise'). The vowel of C_2 is /a/ unless the imperfect stem of the verb has /i/. Many of these forms are simply verbal nouns: /maεrifah/ 'knowledge'.

(2) $miC_1C_2aC_3(ah)$ or $miC_1C_2\bar{a}C_3$ indicate an instrument:

/miftāḥ/ 'key, opener' (/fataḥ/ 'open'); these forms, along with a form with /ī/ in the second syllable, appear as intensive adjectives in a few frozen forms, although the pattern is not productive: /miskīn/ 'poor, wretched'.

(3) $maC_1C_2\bar{u}C_3$ is the passive participle of the simple form of the verb: /maktūb/ 'that which is written, letter'. The /m/ prefix is used throughout the system of derived verbs for participles, nouns of time and place, and auxiliary verbal nouns, but the vowel system is less flexible and the forms are not as clearly differentiated.

(b) *Prefix /t-/*

The form $taC_1C_2v/\bar{v}C_3$ is quite common, but there is no specific association of meaning with nouns with the prefix /ta-/ except as verbal nouns of some derived verbs. Otherwise, these forms appear intermittently as verbal nouns, sometimes being transferred to the agent of the action as intensive adjectives.

(c) *Prefix /ˀ-/*

Outside of the system of derived verbs, the prefixed glottal stop has three principal uses: (a) in forming several different plurals, especially the 'plurals of paucity'; (b) for the comparative-superlative $^{ʔ}aC_1C_2aC_3$, which has the feminine $C_1uC_2C_3\bar{a}$: /ˀaḥsanu rajulin/ 'the fairest of men', /lmalikatu ljumlā/ 'the most beautiful queen'; both diptotes; (c) for adjectives denoting colors or physical peculiarities, with the form $^{ʔ}aC_1C_2aC_3$ in the masculine and $C_1aC_2C_3\bar{a}^{ʔ}$ in the feminine; both diptotes: /ˀaḥdab/ 'hunchbacked (masc. sing.)'; /ˀaṣamm/ (← *ˀaṣmam, root *ṣmm*) 'deaf (masc. sing.)'; /ḥamrāˀ/ 'red (fem. sing.)'.

(d) *Suffix /-ā/*

$C_1aC_2C_3\bar{a}$ is the plural of a number of adjectives of various forms indicating injuries or defects: /marīḍ/ 'sick' pl. /marḍā/: and the feminine of adjectives with suffixed /-ān/: /kaslān/ 'lazy' fem. /kaslā/. (See above for $C_1uC_2C_3\bar{a}$ as the feminine of $^{ʔ}aC_1C_2aC_3$.) $C_1vC_2C_3\bar{a}$

produces a number of verbal nouns: /daεwā/ from /daεā/ 'call', root *dεw*; /d̲ikrā/ from /d̲akar/ 'remember, mention'.

(e) *Suffix /-āˀ/*

This is an inflectional form, yielding the feminine of adjectives for colors and physical peculiarities (see above), and two plurals, both used for nouns denoting rational beings /wazīr/ 'minister' pl. /wuzarāˀ/, /qarīb/ 'relative' pl. /ˀaqribāˀ/.

(f) *Suffix /-ān/*

C_1i/uC_2C_3ān is a plural: /ˀixwān/ 'brothers', /fursān/ 'horsemen'. C_1a/uC_2C_3ān (with /a/, sometimes a diptote) refers to the agent of the verb: /nadmān/ 'penitent'. C_1i/uC_2C_3ān or C_1aC_2aC_3ān are verbal nouns: /šukrān/ 'thanks', /hayajān/ 'agitation'.

(g) *Suffix /-īy-/*

This suffix is added to nouns, especially loanwords, to form relative adjectives which may be used as nouns: /miṣr/ 'Egypt' /miṣrīy/ 'Egyptian, an Egyptian'. When the feminine ending is added, a feminine ('an Egyptian woman'), a collective, or an abstract noun is produced: /qawm/ 'nation', /qawmīy/ 'national', /qawmīyah/ 'nationalism'. This is an extremely productive form, for although the classical grammarians defined a number of complex rules for affixing /-īy/, modern Arab writers ignore many of them, so that, in effect, this suffix can be used with virtually no attention to the internal structure of the word.

(h) *Feminine ending*

The feminine suffix /-at-/ has been mentioned in a wide variety of contexts, and only its major uses will be reiterated here.

Most noun forms which can refer to female beings, particularly the verbal adjectives, can receive this suffix (note that the other types of feminines are limited to specific derivational patterns); most forms of verbal nouns occur with the feminine ending, sometimes with the specification of doing the action once; and most collectives are made singular by adding it. Intensive adjectives are made more intensive by the feminine, and it occurs in a number of plurals, especially those referring to rational beings, or containing semivowels in the root.

1.33 *The Arabic number system*

The Arabs use a system of numbers that work on the same principle as those that we call Arabic, but with different orthographic forms: they are called Indian by the Arabs, after the earlier borrowing, and are written in the same decimal order (from left to right) as our own. The inflection of these numbers—formed on ancient roots which are limited to this subsection of the morphology—and of nouns accompanying them, is handled gingerly, if at all, even by highly educated Arabs.

'One' /wāḥid/, fem. /wāḥidah/, and 'two' /tnān/, fem. /tnatān/, are excepted from the general number system; they are adjectives and follow the noun, agreeing with it in gender, number (/tnān/ is a dual form), definiteness, and case; 3-10 also have masculine and feminine forms, working on a principle which is apparently the opposite of that used for nouns: /sabεah/ 'seven (masc.)', /sabε/ 'seven (fem.)'; 11-19 retain this gender for the digits, followed by a special form of the noun 'ten' whose apparent gender *agrees* with that of the noun: /εašarah/ 'ten (mas.)', /εašr/ 'ten (fem.)'; /εašar/ '-teen (mas.)', /εašrah/ '-teen (fem.)'. These numbers, i.e. 11-19, are undeclinable, being supplied with final /-(t)a/: /sabεata εašara/ 'seventeen (masc.)'; 20 has the unexpected form /εišrūn/, but all the other multiples of ten are simply the sound masculine plurals of the digits, e.g. /sabεūn/ 'seventy', with no gender difference. The words for a hundred, /miˀah/ (no plural in this context) and a thousand, /ˀalf/ (pl. /ˀālāf/) are treated like normal nouns, one masculine and the other feminine; they can be multiplied ('seven hundreds'), or appear in the singular or the dual.

The major difficulty with the numbers is syntactic, and becomes very complex when they are compounded, depending on the role of the object being enumerated in the sentence. In compound numbers, each form is linked to the following one by the conjunction /wa-/ 'and', e.g. /miˀatun wa-sabεūna/ '170', except the two portions of the numbers between 11 and 19. These forms, and the forms for 21-99 (excluding simple multiples of ten), are cited in the reverse order of magnitude: the 'tens' following the 'units', e.g. 'seventeen', 'seven and seventy'. The case and number of the noun are determined by the last number form in the series: the relationship is either a special frozen syntactic pattern (noun in accusative singular) or the normal relationship between a noun (here a number), which has the case appropriate to its position in the sentence, and a following determining complement (the noun enumerated) in the genitive (see 1.73). Number forms which take immediately following nouns as determining complements, e.g. /ˀarbaεatu rijālin/ 'four men', become indefinite when another digit follows, establishing its own relationship with the noun, e.g. /ˀarbaεatun wa-ˀarbaεūna rajulan/ 'four and forty men'.

The forms of the noun are as follows:

	Last number form:
Accusative singular	13-99 (incl.)
Genitive (determining complement following number with sentence case)	
(a) *Singular*	100, 1000 (+ round multiples of either)
(b) *Plural*	3-10

Examples (with full context forms): /sabεatu mulūkin/ '7 kings', /sabεu malikātin/ '7 queens'; /sabεata εašara malikan/ '17 kings', /sabεa εašrata malikatan/ '17 queens'; /sabεatun wa-sabεūna malikan/ '77 kings', /sabεun wa-sabεūna malikatan/ '77 queens'; /sabεatu ˀālāfin wa-sabεu miˀatin wa-sabεatun wa-sabεūna malikan/ '7,777 kings'; /qabla miˀatayni wa-sabεīna malikan/ 'before 270 kings'; /ˀalfā malikatin wa-malikatun (wāḥidatun)/ '2,001 queens'.

For long numbers, especially dates, the order may be: digits, tens, hundreds, thousands. Note that this order corresponds with the fact that the written ciphers follow a left to right sequence.

The roots that form the digits are used for the final digit of ordinals, in the form of active participles: /sābiε/ 'seventh (masc.)'; and for fractions, distributive numbers, etc.: /subε/ or /subuε/ 'one seventh', /subāεīy/ 'consisting of seven parts, seven by seven', /sabbaε/ 'he made sevenfold, divided in seven parts', etc.

1.4 The verb

Arabic has a rich and flexible verb system which is far more regular and predictable than the noun system. Person, aspect, and mode are indicated primarily by affixes; internal patterning produces a number of derived forms which are intensive, causative, reflexive, etc., each derived form being associated with a set of participles and verbal nouns; a further system of vowel shifts differentiates active and passive verbs.

1.41 *Verbal inflection*

Arabic has two sets of verb forms, traditionally called perfect and imperfect. The perfect refers to past time (or completed action) and the imperfect to present or future time (and incompleted action): /katab/ 'he wrote, he has written', /yaktub/ 'he writes, he is writing, he will write'. Finer distinctions are indicated by the use of particles and auxiliary verbs. For both sets of forms, the categories of gender and number are retained, but are not fully indicated for all three persons. A partial set of duals is formed by adding /-ā/ to the masc. and fem. third person singular in both tenses, and to the masc. second person singular (in the imperfect) and plural (in the perfect), or, if this creates an impossible form, to the reconstructed form on which these persons are based. The perfect indicates all categories by means of suffixes, while the imperfect makes a partially realized distinction between the use of prefixes, for person, and suffixes, similar to the nominal suffixes, for gender and number. The imperfect has a further set of endings indicating mode (which does not occur with perfect verbs) and is used without prefixes for the imperative.

1.411 *Person, gender, and number*

The person, gender, and number affixes of the verb are shown in Table 3. Simple, underived verbs have the perfect base $C_1aC_2vC_3$-: /šaribtum/ 'you (masc. pl.) drank'. The third person sing. masc. is the standard dictionary form: /kataba/ 'he wrote', often glossed simply 'write'. The imperfect base is -$C_1C_2vC_3$-, with /a/ in the prefix: /yaktub-/, /tašrabū-/, etc.

In the base forms of simple verbs (see 1.421), all three short vowels occur in both tenses. The number of possible vowels is somewhat simplified for 'weak' verbs (containing a semivowel), and the choice of vowels for the two aspects is more closely related.

1.412 *Mode*

The imperfect is called by the Arabs /lmuḍāriɛ/ 'the resembling [form]' because the three modes are said to resemble the cases of the noun. They are traditionally called the indicative, the subjunctive, and the jussive (a case with a very limited use related to the imperative); they have the following endings:

	After -C_3	*After -$\bar{v}$*	*After -v*
Indicative	-u	-na (fem. & pl.) -ni (dual)	zero
Subjunctive	-a	zero	zero
Jussive (Imperative)	zero/-(i)	zero	zero

The similarity to the noun system is based on the fact that the jussive, when it ends in a consonant, may be supplied with /i/ to resolve a following consonant cluster. The positive imperative is simply the second person form of the jussive stripped of prefixes, with the resulting cluster (if any) resolved (see 1.23): /ˀuktub/ 'write'. (masc. sing.)', /ˀišrabna/ 'drink! (fem. pl.)'.

Table 3

Person, Number, and Gender Affixes of the Verb

PERFECT		IMPERFECT
3rd person		
masc. sing.	/-a/	/ya/u-/
fem. sing.	/-at/	/ta/u-/
masc. pl.	/-ū/	/ya/u--ū-/
fem. pl.	/-na/	/ya/u--na/
masc. dual	/-ā/	/ya/u--ā-/
fem. dual	/-atā/	/ta/u--ā-/
2nd person		
masc. sing.	/-ta/	/ta/u-/
fem. sing.	/-ti/	/ta/u--ī-/
masc. pl.	/-tum/	/ta/u--ū-/
fem. pl.	/-tunna/	/ta/u--na/
dual	/-tumā/	/ta/u--ā-/
1st person		
sing.	/tu/	/ˀa/u-/
pl.	/-na¯/	/na/u-/

Examples: indic. /yaktubu/ 'he writes', subj. /yaktuba/ 'that he write'; indic. /yašrabāni/ 'they two (masc.) drink', subj. /yašrabā/ 'that they two (masc.) drink'.

A further set of suffixes, called 'energetic', may be added to the jussive or imperative: /-(a)n(na/i)/: /yaktuban/, yaktubanna/ third person masc. sing. These forms are complicated and are rarely used.

1.413 *Roots with* C_1 = /ˀ/ or V̭

Roots with initial /ˀ/ are simplified according to the rule that *ˀvˀ- becomes /ˀv̄-/: /ˀākulu/ ← *ˀaˀkulu 'I eat'; the initial /ˀ/ is often lost in the imperative: /kul/ 'eat'. In other parts of the root, the glottal stop behaves regularly (though it presents some difficulty in learning Arabic because there are different ways of writing it).

C_1 = /w/ drops in the primary form of high frequency roots between /a/ and C_2: /yajidu/ 'he finds' ← *yawjidu, root *wjd*. Elsewhere, the resulting possible combinations for initial weak verbs retain the short vowel and semivowel before long vowels, but reduce them to possible long vowels or diphthongs before consonants, the semivowel assimilating to the vowel. C_1 = /w/ assimilates to an infixed /t/ (see 1.422).

1.414 *Roots with C_2 = V̭ or C_3*

C_2 = /y/ has one possible set of bases: C_1ayiC_3- and -C_1yiC_3-; C_2 = /w/ has two possible sets of bases: C_1awuC_3-/-C_1wuC_3- and C_1awiC_3-/-C_1waC_3-. In their inflection and derivation, clusters of vowels and semivowels are formed, which are simplified as follows: (a) /i/, /u/ of C_1 + V̭ + vC_3 → v̄C_3; (b) /a/ + V̭ + vC_3 → /āC_3/, except in the primary verb in those persons of the perfect which have suffixes beginning with a consonant (i.e. in closed syllables), which follow rule (a); (c) a semivowel that is doubled or preceded by a long vowel retains its form, except in the active participle of primary verbs (*qāwim → /qāʾim/ 'standing') and in verbal nouns (/i/ + V̭ + āC_3 → iyāC_3; C + V̭ + āC_3 → CāC_3). As always, where these processes produce long vowels in closed syllables, the vowel is shortened. Examples of the three types (in order): /yabīεu/ 'he buys' (indic.), /yabiε/ (juss.), /bāεa/ 'he bought'—but /biεtu/ 'I bought'; /yaqūmu/ 'he gets up', /yaqum/, /qāma/, /qumtu/; /yanāmu/ 'he sleeps', /yanam/, /nāma/, /nimtu/.

Where two identical last consonants of a root (i.e. C_2 = C_3) are separated by a short vowel, as -C_2vC_3, they are rearranged wherever the surrounding syllable structure will permit, as -(v)C_2C_3- throughout the verb system and in nouns directly derived from verbs (e.g. not in plurals: /judud/, 'new (pl.)'); in participles: /ḍāll/ ← *ḍālil (the commonest source of overlong syllables); nouns of place: /maḥall/ 'place' ← *maḥlal; comparatives: /ʾahamm/ 'more important' ← *ʾahmam, etc. This results in the following verb forms: /radda/ 'he returned'—but /radadta/ 'you (masc. sing.) returned'; /yaruddu/ 'he returns' (indic.)—but, in the jussive, /yardud/. Note that since the same factors of syllable structure are operating, the same persons that have /v̄/ if C_2 = V̭ , have a doubled consonant if $C_2 = C_3$: /yaqūmu/, /yaruddu/; while those which have a short vowel separate the consonants: /qumta/, /radadta/.

1.415 *Roots with C_3 = V̭*

C_3 = /w/ has one principle set of bases: C_1aC_2aw-/-C_1C_2uw-; C_3 = /y/ has two: C_1aC_2ay-/-C_1C_2iy and C_1aC_2iy-/-C_1C_2ay-. These bases are handled as follows:

(a) for any suffix beginning with a long vowel, the correspon-ding semivowel replaces C_3, and the short vowel of the suffix is lost:

> mašay- + -ū (= -uw) → /mašaw/ 'they (masc.) walked': $\frac{\text{ay-}}{\text{-uw}}$;
>
> tadεuw- + -ī na (= -iyna) → *tadεuyna → /tadεī na/ 'you (fem. sing.) call': $\frac{\text{uw-}}{\text{-iy}}$;

(b) phonologically excluded vowel-semivowel clusters, i.e. all but the long /ī/ and /ū/, which may be followed by /a/ or /ā/ (iyā⃡, uwā⃡), and the diphthongs, which may be followed by /ā/, are simplified and reduced by the assimila-tion of a preceding /i/ or /u/ (and any vowels following the cluster) to the semivowel (→ /ī/ or /ū/), or of the semivowel to preceding /a/:

> /tadεuwa/ 'that you (masc. sing.) call' (subj.);
> /tadεawta/ 'you (masc. sing.) called';
> /tamšī/ 'you (masc. sing.) walk' ← *tamšiyu;—but
> /mašā/ 'he walked' ← *mašaya;

(c) when the result in the jussive is a final long vowel that does not indicate gender or number, it is shortened:

	indic.	*subj.*	*juss.*
you (masc. sing.)	/tadεū̱/	/tadεu̱wa/	/tadεu̱/
you (fem. sing.)	/tadεī na/	/tadεī/	/tadεī/

(d) further changes may of course be required by the syllable structure:

/mašat/ 'she walked' ← *mašāt ← *mašayat.

Complex as these rules are, they are applied with great regularity, although they result in the loss of a number of distinctions, e.g. /yadεūna/, 'they call' results from both *yadεuwūna (masc. pl. imperf.) and *yadεuwna (fem. pl. imperf.). Furthermore, the similarity of the imperfect verb and the noun comes in surprisingly handy here: the final syllables of those persons of the imperfect for C_3 = /y/ which do not have suffixes for gender and number correspond closely to the case endings of definite nouns with final C_3 = /y/. For the derived verbs, the vowel preceding C_3 is part of an invariable pattern (always /a/ or /i/) and C_3 = V̭ is always treated as /y/, so that the relationship between the final syllable and the suffixes may be handled without any reference to changes earlier in the word. Like C_2 = V̭, C_3 = V̭ becomes /ˀ/ after /ā/ (i.e. in the verbal nouns of derived verbs). Table 4 should clarify the application of these rules (only part of the conjugation is shown, from which the remainder may easily be inferred).

1.42 ***Verbal derivation***

As in the case of the nouns, Arabic verbs show a progressive movement from the simple form, containing only the three root consonants and short vowels, which has been considered thus far, to much more complex forms produced by lengthening vowels or consonants or by adding consonantal elements. However, the verb system differs from the noun system in that after the first derivational step beyond the primary verbs, which have a number of possible vowel patterns, each derived form appears with only one possible vowel pattern. However, the

Table 4

Conjugation of Verbs with Roots with C_3 = V̭

dɛw 'call'		*mšy* 'walk'	*bqy* 'remain'
Perfect	C_1aC_2aw-	*Perfect* C_1aC_2ay-	*Perfect* C_1aC_2iy-
3 m.s.	/daɛā/	/mašā/	/baqiya/
3 f.s.	/daɛat/	/mašat/	/baqiyat/
3 m.pl.	/daɛaw/	/mašaw/	/baqū/
3 f.pl.	/daɛawna/	/mašayna/	/baqīna/
3 m.d.	/daɛawā/	/mašayā/	/baqiyā/
3 f.d.	/daɛatā/	/mašatā/	/baqiyatā/
2 m.s.	/daɛawta/	/mašayta/	/baqīta/
Imperf. Indic.	-C_1C_2uw-	*Imperf.* -C_1C_2iy-	*Imperf.* -C_1C_2ay-
2 m.s.	/tadɛū/	/tamšī/	/tabqā/
2 f.s.	/tadɛīna/	/tamšīna/	/tabqayna/
2 m.pl.	/tadɛūna/	/tamšūna/	/tabqawna/
2 f.pl.	/tadɛūna/	/tamšīna/	/tabqayna/
2 m.d.	/tadɛuwāni/	/tamšiyāni/	/tabqayāni/
Jussive			
2 m.s.	/tadɛu/	/tamši/	/tabqa/
Subjunctive			
2 m.s.	/tadɛuwa/	/tamšiya/	/tabqā/

vowel patterns of both primary and derived verbs may give way to an additional pattern, that of the passive, which is constant throughout.

1.421 *The formation of primary verbs*

Primary verbs in Arabic have the stem $C_1aC_2vC_3$- in the perfect, and -$C_1C_2vC_3$- in the imperfect. They always have /a/ in the first syllable of the perfect, and in the imperfect they use prefixes containing /a/. The variable short vowels of primary verbs—marked by the symbol (v)—must be lexically specified in each case. For the 'weak' verbs, the system is distorted, so that there are only a few possibilities, and these may be arbitrarily specified to provide for the simplest formal statement of the behavior of particular groups of verbs. All other verbs seem to reflect some ancient derivational process without being perfectly regular, since they have been disrupted by analogies and semantic shift. Even among the verbs which do not have weak C_2 or C_3, certain phonological conditions can interfere with the derivational pattern, but they must be described as deviations from it. The semantic content is attached primarily to the vowel of the perfect, which is only a partial basis for predicting the vowel of the imperfect.

1. short /a/ in the perfect: $C_1aC_2aC_3$- (usually transitive):
   (a) imperfect -$C_1C_2uC_3$-; this is the commonest form of primary verb: /katab yaktub/ 'write', /qatal yaqtul/ 'kill, murder';
   (b) imperfect -$C_1C_2iC_3$-; may denote briefer or more superficial actions than the preceding form: /ḍarab yaḍrib/ 'hit';
2. short /i/ in the perfect; $C_1aC_2iC_3$- (usually intransitive, often expressing a temporary state, including the holding of an opinion or attitude); imperfect -$C_1C_2aC_3$-: /fariḥ yafraḥ/ 'rejoice', /ḥasib yaḥsab/ 'think, consider';
3. short /u/ in the perfect; $C_1aC_2uC_3$- (usually intransitive, expressing a permanent state or the acquisition of a lasting trait); imperfect -$C_1C_2uC_3$-: /qabuḥ yaqbuḥ/ 'be ugly', /ḥasun yaḥsun/ 'be beautiful'.

The principal phonological factors disrupting this are (a) the existence of an additional pattern with v=/a/ for both aspects, which is followed only by verbs with C_2 or C_3 = a back consonant, i.e. /ġ × ε ḥ ʾ h/: /baεaṯ yabεaṯ/ 'send'; (b) if C_1 = /w/, verbs of type 1(a) have /i/ in the imperfect: /wajad yajid/ 'find'; and verbs of type 1(b) have /i/ in the perfect as well: /wariṯ yariṯ/ 'inherit'.

A further factor of asymmetry is the increased tendency to use prepositions with verbs of motion which were originally transitive and have transitive vowel patterns. However, the distinctions do have some reality: /ḥazan yaḥzun/ 'sadden' vs. /ḥazin yaḥzan/ 'be sad, grieve'; /kabar yakbur/ 'exceed (someone) in age' vs. /kabur yakbur/ 'become great'; /safil yasfal/ 'be low' vs. /saful yasful/ 'be base, despicable'.

1.422 *Derived verbs*

Arabic has some fourteen derived verb forms, only ten of which will concern us here, the remainder being very rare and unproductive. In the perfect, all have /a/ or /ā/ throughout, except where other vowels are introduced in the regular manner to resolve initial clusters. In the imperfect, each form is characterized by its first vowel, i.e. by the use of /a/ or /u/ with the personal prefixes, and by the vowel following C_2; all other vowel positions that occur are filled by /a/ or /ā/. The traditional Arabic order of the forms which concern us here (Forms II-XI) is unilluminating from the point of view of content, etymology or syllabic structure; it is, however, designed to illuminate the different vowel patterns of the imperfect (see Table 5).

The three columns in Table 5 provide some information on other forms of the verbs: the perfects may be formed for the second column simply by stripping off the third person prefix of the imperfect, while for the first and third columns, all the vowels must be changed to /a/ and, for the third, an anaptyctic vowel and glottal stop provided: (ʾi)nCaCaC-, (ʾi)CtaCaC-, etc. The same base acts as verbal noun for Forms V and VI, with the change of the vowel of C_2 to /u/; and for Forms VII-X, with the first stem vowel changed to /i/ and the last to /ā/:

Table 5

Vowel Patterns of the Imperfect of the Derived Verbs

u---i	a---a	a---i
II $yuC_1aC_2C_2iC_3$-	V $yataC_1aC_2C_2aC_3$-	VII $yanC_1aC_2iC_3$-
III $yuC_1\bar{a}C_2iC_3$-	VI $yataC_1\bar{a}C_2aC_3$-	VIII $yaC_1taC_2iC_3$-
IV $yuC_1C_2iC_3$-		IX $*yaC_1C_2aC_3iC_3$- $\rightarrow yaC_1C_2aC_3C_3$-
		X $yastaC_1C_2iC_3$-
		XI $*yaC_1\ C_2\bar{a}C_3iC_3$- $\rightarrow$ yaC1C2āC3C3-

$taC_1aC_2C_2uC_3$, $(^{ʔ}i)C_1tiC_2\bar{a}C_3$, $(^{ʔ}i)stiC_1C_2\bar{a}C_3$, etc. The items in the first column have the following forms:

Perfect	*Verbal noun*
II $C_1aC_2C_2aC_3$-	$taC_1C_2\bar{i}C_3$
III $C_1\bar{a}C_2aC_3$-	$C_1iC_2\bar{a}C_3$ or $muC_1\bar{a}C_2aC_3ah$
IV $^{ʔ}aC_1C_2aC_3$-	$^{ʔ}iC_1C_2\bar{a}C_3$

A structural examination of the derived verb forms shows that four of them, Forms II, III, IX, and XI, are produced without additional consonantal elements: by lengthening a vowel, by doubling C_2, or by doubling C_3. Form IV has a prefixed /ʔ/ in the perfect: $^{ʔ}aC_1C_2C_3$-; while Form VII has a prefixed /n/. All of the remaining forms have a prefixed or infixed /t/, with the general effect of making the form less transitive, often reflexive or reciprocal.

more transitive	*less transitive*
I $C_1aC_2vC_3$-/$yaC_1C_2vC_3$-	VIII $(^{ʔ}i)C_1taC_2aC_3$-/$yaC_1taC_2iC_3$-
II $C_1aC_2C_2aC_3$-/$yuC_1aC_2C_2iC_3$-	V $taC_1aC_2C_2aC_3$-/$yataC_1aC_2C_2aC_3$-
III $C_1\bar{a}C_2aC_3$-/$yuC_1\bar{a}C_2iC_3$-	VI $taC_1\bar{a}C_2aC_3$-/$yataC_1\bar{a}C_2aC_3$-
IV $^{ʔ}aC_1C_2aC_3$-/$yuC_1C_2iC_3$-	X $(^{ʔ}i)staC_1C_2aC_3$-/$yastaC_1C_2iC_3$-

However, the forms have acquired other connotations, and some of the relationships are only of historical and etymological interest, e.g. the /ˀ/ of Form IV is historically related to the /s/ of Form X.

SUMMARY OF DERIVED VERBS AND THEIR MEANINGS

The following primary verbs serve as references for overlapping examples of the relationships between simple and derived forms: /ɛalim/ 'know', /ḥasun/ 'be good, beautiful', /kaḏab/ 'lie', /katab/ 'write', /šaġal/ 'occupy', /qatal/ 'kill'. In the summary below, prosthetic syllables are indicated in parentheses for the canonical forms but omitted in the examples.

II $C_1aC_2C_2aC_3$-, $yuC_1aC_2C_2iC_3$-, $taC_1C_2\bar{i}C_3$:
- (a) to do intensively or repeatedly: /qattal/ 'massacre', /šaġġal/ 'engross, employ';
- (b) to cause to do: /ɛallam/ 'teach';
- (c) to believe or declare something is done: /kaḏḏab/ 'accuse of lying, refute'.

III $C_1\bar{a}C_2aC_3$-, $yuC_1\bar{a}C_2iC_3$-, $muC_1\bar{a}C_2aC_3ah$ ~ $C_1iC_2\bar{a}C_3$:
- (a) to endeavor to do something: /qātal/ 'fight with and try to kill';
- (b) to direct an action or quality toward someone: /kātab/ 'write to', /ḥāsan/ 'treat kindly' (if Form I requires a preposition, Form III is directly transitive).

IV $ˀaC_1C_2aC_3$-, $yuC_1C_2iC_3$-, $ˀiC_1C_2\bar{a}C_3$:
- (a) to cause to do: /ˀaɛlam/ 'inform', /ˀaktab/ 'dictate', /ˀakḏab/ 'cause to lie';
- (b) to believe or declare something is done: /ˀakḏab/ 'call or prove a liar';
- (c) to characterize to an extraordinary degree (with /mā/; used in third person perf. only): /mā ˀaḥsanahu/ 'how handsome he is!'

V $taC_1aC_2C_2aC_3$-, $yataC_1aC_2C_2aC_3$-, $taC_1aC_2C_2uC_3$: to become, to enter the state cause by II(b) or do it to oneself; /taɛallam/ 'become learned', /taḥassan/ 'improve, become better'.

VI $taC_1\bar{a}C_2aC_3$-, $yataC_1\bar{a}C_2aC_3$-, $taC_1\bar{a}C_2uC_3$:
(a) to pretend or simulate: /tašāġal/ 'pretend to be busy';
(b) to act mutually: /taqātal/· 'fight with each other', /takātab/ 'correspond'.

VII $(^{?}i)nC_1aC_2aC_3$-, $yanC_1aC_2iC_3$-, $(^{?}i)nC_1iC_2\bar{a}C_3$: to have (or allow to be) done to oneself: /nšaġal/ 'be occupied, kept busy'.

VIII $(^{?}i)C_1taC_2aC_3$-, $yaC_1taC_2iC_3$-, $(^{?}i)C_1tiC_2\bar{a}C_3$: reflexive of I: /ktatab/ 'be registered, recorded; copy': /qtatal/ 'fight with each other'.

IX $(^{?}i)C_1C_2aC_3C_3$-, $yaC_1C_2aC_3C_3$-, $(^{?}i)C_1C_2iC_3\bar{a}C_3$: to become characterized by a particular color or physical defect: /ḥmarr/ 'become red', /εwajj/ 'become crooked'.

X $(^{?}i)staC_1C_2aC_3$-, $yastaC_1C_2iC_3$-, $(^{?}i)stiC_1C_2\bar{a}C_3$:
(a) to ask someone to do something: /staktab/ 'ask someone to write';
(b) reflexive of IV: /staεlam/ 'inquire, seek information';
(c) to attribute a quality: /staḥsan/ 'consider good, admire, sanction'.

XI $(^{?}i)C_1C_2\bar{a}C_3C_3$-, $yaC_1C_2\bar{a}C_3C_3$-, $(^{?}i)C_1C_2\bar{i}C_3\bar{a}C_3$: a rare form identical in meaning with IX: /ˀaswādd/ 'become black'.

Even in this idealized form, it is clear that the system is far from rigid: Forms II and IV, IX and XI, as well as Forms VI, VII, and VIII, show immediate possibilities of overlap; most forms have additional specialized usages not mentioned here; and most derivations from the primary form depend on whether the primary form is transitive or not. Roots generally appear in only three or four forms, but further derived forms may be coined. Anciently coined forms have often drifted into meanings which seem totally arbitrary or have become highly specific.

Nominal roots may be given different kinds of verbal meaning by verbal derivation, usually in the following patterns:

II to become or be occupied with something: /šarraq/ 'go east' (cf. /šarq/ 'east');

IV to produce something, pretend to be something: /ʾamṭar/ 'produce rain' (cf. /maṭar/ 'rain'); /ʾaqfar/ 'become desert' (cf. /qafr/ 'desert');

X to ask for something: /stamṭar/ 'ask for rain'.

1.4221 *Passive verbs*

All of these forms, except Forms VII, IX and XI, may be put into the passive voice, as may the first form. Passive verbs have, in the perfect, the vowel sequence u---i, with the /i/ directly preceding C_3, and /u/ or /ū/ in all other positions in the stem: Form I $C_1uC_2iC_3$-; Form V $tuC_1uC_2C_2iC_3$-; Form X (ʾu)$stuC_1C_2iC_3$-; etc., and in the imperfect, by the sequence u---a, with /u/ for the personal prefix and /a/ or /ā/ throughout the stem: Form X $yustaC_1C_2aC_3$-.

In addition to the verbal nouns, active and passive participles may be derived from all these forms: this is most simply schematized if passive participles are shown by substituting /m/ for the consonant of the personal prefix of the imperfect passive, and active participles by changing the vowel before C_3 to /i/:

	Imp. Active	*Imp. Passive*	*Pass. partic.*	*Act. partic.*
II	$yuC_1aC_2C_2iC_3$-	$yuC_1aC_2C_2aC_3$-	$muC_1aC_2C_2aC_3$	$muC_1aC_2C_2iC_3$
V	$yataC_1aC_2C_2aC_3$-	$yutaC_1aC_2C_2aC_3$-	$mutaC_1aC_2C_2aC_3$	$mutaC_1aC_2C_2iC_3$
X	$yastaC_1C_2iC_3$-	$yustaC_1C_2aC_3$-	$mustaC_1C_2aC_3$	$mustaC_1C_2iC_3$

This is the case by analogy even if the intervening forms do not occur:

VII	$yanC_1aC_2iC_3$-	*$yunC_1aC_2aC_3$-	*$munC_1aC_2aC_3$	$munC_1aC_2iC_3$

In the derived systems, the multitude of nouns that were described as generally related to the primary verbs are replaced by the three-way system of verbal noun and active and passive participles: all agents and adjectives are expressed by the participles, and the passive participles have the additional functions of nouns of time and place and of alternate verbal nouns.

1.5 Non-triliteral forms

1.51 *Biliteral forms*

Arabic has inherited from Proto-Semitic a number of biliteral roots which retain a marginal place in the noun system, e.g. /yad/ 'hand', as well as traces of even briefer forms which must be padded to function at all and may have a number of variants: /fv̄ (nom. fū, gen. fī, accus. fā)/ ~ / fam/ 'mouth'. Before such roots may be used freely in the derivational system, they must have at least three elements, and many of them have forms in which a /y/ or a /w/ is supplied: /dam/ 'blood', /damiya/ 'bleed'. Because only a small number of genuinely biliteral nouns survive, it is impossible to say how many of the weak verbs of Arabic may originally have been biliteral. One theory maintains the biliteral origin of all Semitic roots, pointing to the existence of series of roots with two consonants (or even one consonant) and semantic content in common.

1.52 *Quadriliteral forms: derived nouns and verbs*

Both in the noun system and in the verb system, the presence of forms with derivational consonantal affixes and, even more conspicuously, with doubled consonants, means that Arabic has patterns for handling roots with four consonants. For example, the formation of such nouns as /farrūj/ 'chick', root *frj*, /maktūb/ 'letter', root *ktb*, and /dukkān/ 'shop', root *dkk*, all having the general pattern CvCCv̄C and plural CaCāCīC with the actual three consonants of the root variously distributed, allows the language to handle such nouns as /burhān/ 'proof', pl. /barāhīn/, root *brhn*. Nouns derived from quadriliteral roots are quite common in Arabic, but their variety is limited to forms which can be seen as variants of patterns existing within the triliteral system. The same may be said of the verb system, so that the Form I verb from a quadriliteral root behaves precisely like the Form II verb of a triliteral root: /barhan yubarhin/, etc., except for the verbal noun, which usually follows the nominal pattern CvCCāC, using all the consonantal slots for members of the root. By the same token, the second quadriliteral form corresponds to the triliteral Form V: /tafalsaf/ 'philosophize, pretend to be a philosopher'. The /n/ affix of the triliteral Form VII is infixed to provide a Form III for the quadriliteral system, whose vowel-consonant pattern (ˀi)CCanCaC corresponds to the triliteral Form X pattern (ˀi)sta$C_1C_2aC_3$: /branšaq yabranšiq/ 'blossom, flourish', root *bršq*. A rare fourth form exists, (ˀi)$C_1C_2aC_3aC_4C_4$, roughly corresponding in pattern to a specialized development of the triliteral Form XI, and in derivation to Form IX.

1.53 *The development of quadriliteral forms*

An examination of the relationship between roots with three and four consonants reveals the following types of quadriliteral roots:

(a) quadriliteral roots that can be traced to triliteral ones:
  (1) with a repetition of C_1: $C_1C_2C_1C_3$ /qahqar/ 'fall back, retreat', cf. /qahar/ 'defeat';
  (2) with dissimilation of doubled C_2: $C_1C_NC_2C_3$ /faqqaɛ/, /farqaɛ/ both 'crack, snap'; C_N may be /r l n y w/;
  (3) with an added fourth consonant: $C_1C_2C_3C_N$ /šamxar/ 'be lofty'; C_N may be /r l s/; cf. /šamax/ 'be lofty';
  (4) with a consonant which was added as part of an identifiable process of derivation treated as if it belonged to the root: /tama<u>d</u>hab/ 'adhere to a sect', from /ma<u>d</u>hab/ 'sect, way', a noun of place from /<u>d</u>ahab/ 'go'; here $C_NC_1C_2C_3$;

(b) quadriliteral roots that can be traced to biliteral ones: $C_1C_2C_1C_2$ /waswas/ 'whisper'; many such verbs have corresponding forms which are triliteral through the doubling of C_2, or have a third weak consonant: the presence of a few such verbs which seem to parallel forms with three sound consonants supports the biliteral theory; many of these verbs are onomatapoetic: /ġarġar/ 'gargle';

(c) non-reducible quadriliterals $C_1C_2C_3C_4$: many quadriliterals cannot be reduced to basic sets of two or three consonants; some must simply be treated as roots with four consonants, but others may be analyzed in terms of two major processes:

(1) borrowing (often very ancient): /falsaf/ 'philosophize', /ˀamrak/ 'Americanize'; most new quadriliteral verbs belong in this class;
(2) abbreviation: /ṣalεam/ 'say (after any mention of the Prophet Muḥammad): /ṣallā ḷḷāhu εalayhi wasallam/ "God bless him and grant him salvation"'; /basmal/ 'say: /bismi llāh.../ "in the name of God..."'

These processes are all given in terms of verbs, but the development of quadriliterals often takes place in the nominal system first, especially of types (a) and (c(l)). The complex interaction of the forms may be further demonstrated through such clusters as: /zall/ 'slip, slide', /zalaq/ 'glide, slide', /zaḥlaq/ 'roll, slide', /zaḥaf/ 'crawl' (cf. the Hebrew root *ḥlq*, which has one form with the meaning 'smooth'), etc. The interplay of these different roots surely precedes the separate development of Arabic.

1.6 Outside the root system

Besides the two interlocking systems built up of roots and patterns, the verbal and nominal systems, Arabic has a third system of particles. Membership in the class of particles is, on the one hand, a matter of function, since the particles are the words which do much of the grammatical work of the sentence; on the other hand, although ties with the root system are occasionally discernible, particles are words which do not have true roots or true patterns and are not included in the two inflectional systems. In many cases, especially among the pronouns, they seem to be composed of monosyllabic elements strung together (often with alternative long and short forms) to produce words of varying bulk; an analysis from this point of view, especially when it begins to deal with possibilities of relationships between such elements and the consonant affixes of the root-based systems, rapidly becomes speculative and can only be extensive if it is carried out from a comparative or historical point of view. The following section is more concerned with giving a range of examples than with an exhaustive coverage.

1.61 *Monoliteral and biliteral particles*

A small series of particles appear as single unstressed syllables standing before the word. They are less closely bound to the word than the inflectional prefixes, and tend to express syntactic relationships. Among these are the conjunctions /wa-/ 'and' (implying simultaneity) and /fa-/ 'and' (implying sequence); /sa-/, which makes an imperfect verb future; /ˀa-/, an interrogative; /la-/, which adds emphasis; /li-/, which introduces a subjunctive; and the prepositions /bi-/ 'in, by, with', /li- ~ la-/ 'to', /ka-/ 'like', and /wa-/, introducing an oath, which govern the genitive. A further group of slightly more substantial forms includes: /hal/, an interrogative; /law/ 'if'; the prepositions /ɛan/ 'from, about'; /fī/ 'in'; /ˀilā ~ ˀilay-/ 'to, toward'; etc., going on towards forms which contain recognizable roots.

1.62 *Sets of particles*

A second way of looking at the particles isolates a number of families of particles, such as the negations /lā/ for the imperfect, /lam/ (+ verb in the jussive) for the perfect, and /lan/ (+ the subjunctive) for the future. Another such series is formed by the interrogative (relative) pronouns /mā/ and /māḏā/ 'what'; /man/ 'who'; /matā/ 'when'. A series of great syntactic importance is built on the base /n/:

Before verbs	*Before nouns (accus.) or pronouns*
/ˀin/ 'if'	/ˀinna/ 'indeed'
/ˀan/ 'so that'	/ˀanna/ 'that'
/lākin/ 'but'	/lākinna/ 'but'

On this level of complexity, we begin to find a great many particles which are recognizable combinations of two or more particles which exist separately: /kaˀanna/ 'as though' (+ noun); /bilā/ 'without'; /ˀillā/ ← /ˀin/ + /lā/ 'except'; /limāḏā/ 'why'; etc.

1.63 *Pronouns*

An examination of the above forms reveals at once the difficulty of dissecting the particles of Arabic without constant historical references. Between the forms which clearly consist of a single element, and those which are clearly compounded of at least two elements (which still have an autonomous existence, strung together at some early date), are a number of sets of particles which seem related in one or more of their elements but cannot readily be analyzed.

The pronouns of Arabic are of special interest, since they present an extensive system of composite forms, syllables, and single consonants strung together, of varying bulk. In many cases, variants have been retained, e.g. /d̲āka/, /hād̲āka/, /d̲ālika/ (plus the dminutives /d̲ayyāka/ and /d̲ayyālika/) 'that (masc. sing.)', but only the prevailing modern forms are given in the Tables below.

The Arab grammarians have traditionally treated the pronouns with the nouns rather than with the particles, because of their role in the sentence and because they reflect the obligatory categories of the noun (case, gender, and number). However, they resemble the particles in lying outside the root system, and they indicate gender and number differently, often by vowel contrasts: /huwa/ 'he' vs. /hiya/ 'she'.

1.631 *Personal pronouns*

The personal pronouns (Table 6) are quite brief, and have some resemblance to the agent affixes of the verb. They have two forms, an isolated form which generally refers to the subject of the clause and a suffixed form which replaces either the accusative or the genitive and is suffixed to nouns, verbs, and many particles after their final short vowel. Examples of the use of suffixed forms: /ṭalabtu-hum/ 'I sought them', /nusāεidu-ka/ 'we will help you'.

The /-(n)-/ of the first person singular is required after verbs and some particles, while the /-iy(a)/ form is used after nouns and obscures the case ending: /bayt-ī/ 'my house' (case unknown) vs. /ṭalabta-nī/ 'you (masc. sing.) sought me'. The

Table 6

Personal Pronouns

	ISOLATED FORM	SUFFIXED FORM
3rd person		
Masc. sing.	/huwa/	/-hu/(~/-hū/)
Fem. sing.	/hiya/	/-hā/
Masc. pl.	/hum/	/-hum/
Fem. pl.	/hunna/	/-hunna/
Dual	/humā/	/-humā/
2nd person		
Masc. sing.	/ˀanta/	/-ka/
Fem. sing.	/ˀanti/	/-ki/
Masc. pl.	/ˀantum/	/-kum/
Fem. pl.	/ˀantunna/	/-kunna/
Dual	/ˀantumā/	/-kumā/
1st person		
Singular	/ˀanā/	/-(n)iy(a)/
Plural	/naḥnu/	/-nā/

final /-(a)/ is required only when the /-iy-/ elides with a /-y/ at the end of the stem; it is optional and rather old-fashioned elsewhere: /εalay-/ 'on' + /-iy(a)/ → /εalayya/ 'on me'.

The short /u/ of the third person suffixes is replaced by /i/ when it follows /-i/ or /-y/: /bayti-himā/ 'of their (dual) house'.

The suffixed pronouns are determining complements, and the nouns to which they are affixed cannot have nunation or the definite article, while duals and sound masculine plurals lose their final -nv: /muslimī-hi/ 'of his Muslims'.

1.632 *Demonstrative and relative pronouns*

These pronouns, which accompany or replace definite nouns only, are built up from ancient demonstrative elements plus various determining elements and indications of gender and number. The arrangement of the demonstratives /d̲/ (masc.) vs. /t/ (fem.) vs. /1/ (common plural) contrasts with the relative, which retains the /d̲/ vs. /t/ contrast and distinguishes gender in the plural. For the demonstratives, /h/ vs. /k/ expresses near (this) and far (that), and recurs in /hunā/ and /hāhunā/ 'here' vs. /hunāka/, /hunālika/ 'there'. Note also /hākad̲ā/ 'thus'.

The forms given in Table 7 are standard for modern usage, but there are a number of variants—this is one of the areas of Arabic grammar where one is most aware of ancient heterogeneity.

The initial /l/ of the relative pronoun is the definite article, and requires /ˀa-/ after silence (see 1.23). All of the dual forms differentiate between the nominative and other cases by the same vowel alternation as for nouns: /d̲aynnika/ 'those (two)' (gen. or accus.).

In addition to these, Arabic employs the interrogative pronouns as relatives which do not reflect the obligatory categories of the noun (see 1.62); there are others which do not belong to this series, especially /ˀayy/ 'whatever, whoever, which', etc. The suffix /-mā/ often corresponds to English '-ever': /ˀaynamā/ 'wherever'.

1.7 Syntax

Any complete description of Arabic syntax would go far beyond the scope of this structural sketch; for brevity, we must be concerned with interesting or pivotal features of Arabic syntax, rather than with the attempt to present it as a coherent system. We shall be concerned here with (a) the relationship between the three categories (nouns, verbs, and particles) which have been necessary for a formal description of Arabic, and the more elaborate system of 'parts of speech' which might be expected on the basis of a conventional training in

Table 7

Demonstrative and Relative Pronouns

Demonstrative pronouns:

	Singular		*Dual*		*Plural*	
	masc.	*fem.*	*masc.*	*fem.*	*masc.*	*fem.*
'this'	/hāḏā/	/hāḏihi/	/hāḏāni/	/hātāni/	/hāʾulāʾi/	
'that'	/ḏālika/	/tilka/	/ḏānnika/	/tānnika/	/ʾulāʾika/	

Relative pronouns:

'which'	/llaḏī/	/llatī/	/llaḏāni/	/llatāni/	/llaḏīna/	/llāti/

English grammar; (b) the major sentence, clause, and phrase types; and (c) the functions of the case and modal endings.

1.71 *Parts of speech*

Nouns and verbs are distinguished in Arabic (a) derivationally, because different sets of patterns may be ascribed to each class; (b) inflectionally, because different kinds of affixes are joined to each (verbs indicate person, nouns indicate definiteness and case, and there is only a partial similarity between the way the two systems indicate gender and number); and (c) functionally, in terms of the syntactic roles they can play in the sentence.

The role played by the verb has relatively few surprises for the speaker of English: Arabic employs special (usually non-verbal) constructions in place of some English uses of the verb 'to have' and the present of the verb 'to be', and tends to outdo English in using verbs to describe states: Arabic prefers 'he grieves' or 'he rages' to 'he is unhappy', 'he is angry'.

The noun, on the other hand, fills a number of functions which are associated with a greater specialization in English.

Although there is some separation in terms of derivational patterns, the remarks on nominal inflection (see 1.3) apply to words which fill roles corresponding to the following English categories:

(a) Substantives: /b̲ayt/ 'house', /hind/ 'Hind (a woman's name)', /lištirākīyah/ '(the) socialism'.

(b) Adjectives, including participles and comparatives-superlatives: /karīm/ 'noble, generous', /kātib/ 'writing', /ˀakbar/ 'bigger, biggest'. These forms, when used syntactically to express attributes, follow the noun and agree with it in gender, number and determination, but they may also stand alone: /karīm/ 'a noble or generous man, Karīm (a man's name)', /kātib/ 'scribe, secretary', /kātibah/ 'secretary (fem.)', /ˀakbar/ 'Akbar (a man's name)', /lˀakbar/ 'the greatest (one)'. Nor is it useful to speak of an adjectival inflection 'big, bigger, biggest', since comparative-superlative forms often exist in direct relationship with the verb without reference to an adjectival base form. There is some morphological justification for setting up a class of adjectives on the basis of the partial specialization of derivational forms, the ease with which feminine endings may be applied, and the specialization of plurals: participles and relative adjectives generally take sound plurals, and even where they have broken plurals, these are more predictable than broken plurals of nouns. When the use of first form participles as substantives crystallizes, they acquire specialized broken plurals: /rrijālu l-kātibūn/ 'the writing men' vs. /lkuttāb/ 'the scribes'.

(c) Adverbs: In Arabic there is no real class of adverbs corresponding to the English one. Arabic has a number of adverbial particles, e.g. /faqaṭ/ 'only, no more', which follows the verb, but most of the load carried in English by adverbs is carried in Arabic by nouns in the accusative (see 1.72): /lyawm/ 'the day', /lyawma/ 'today'; 'sarīɛ/ 'swift', /sarīɛan/ 'swiftly'; /dāˀim/ 'continuing' (active participle of /dām/ 'continue'), /dāˀiman/ 'always'.

(d) Prepositions: In addition to the monoliteral and biliteral prepositions discussed above (see 1.6), most of the 'prepositions' of Arabic are actually nouns with identifiable roots, which are in the accusative because they are filling an adverbial function and are determined by a following genitive: /qabla ḥarbin/ 'before a war', /fawqa lˀarḍi/ 'above the ground'. The roots appear in other forms: /qabil/ 'receive', /fāq/ 'surpass'; and they may take the diminutive: /fuwayqa lˀarḍi/ 'just above the ground'; or stand alone as adverbs: /qablan/ 'previously'. However, there is some justification for separating a group of these 'prepositions' from the general class of nouns, since they do also appear adverbially with the fossil Semitic adverbial ending /-u/: /qablu/ and even /min qablu/ 'previously'; never take the definite article; and may be followed by /ˀan/ to introduce a clause.

1.72 *Major clause types*

Although Arabic is an inflected language, it does have a relatively rigid word order which allows for stylistic deviations. The two major clause types of Arabic are differentiated by the presence or absence of a verb.

Verbal clauses have the basic order:

$+$ verb $\pm$ subject $\pm$ object $\pm$ adverbial(s)

(a) The form of the verb itself indicates the person of the subject: /qataltu/ 'I killed'; and may include a pronominal object: /qataltu-hu/ 'I killed him'; so that Arabic verbs, unlike English verbs, readily form single-word sentences. No modification need be made in this pattern for passive verbs, except that they do not have direct objects (unless the active form was doubly or triply transitive), since passive verbs in Arabic, unlike those of English, cannot have a stated agent. The verb may be preceded by a conjunction, and the verb position may be filled by a verb phrase consisting of a verb plus one or more particles which normally precede it; the two sets of verb forms (perfect vs. imperfect) provided by the morphology are supplemented by more detailed syntactic indications of present vs. future, especially in negative sentences and within subordinate clauses:

	AFFIRMATIVE	NEGATIVE	
PAST	/qad/ + perf.	/mā/ + perf. /lam/ + juss.	
PRESENT		/mā/ + imperf.	/lā/ + imperf.
FUTURE	/sa-/ + imperf. /sawfa/ + imperf.	/sawfa lā/ + imperf. /lan/ + subj.	

(b) The subject, if it is present, may be a noun or noun phrase, or a personal or demonstrative pronoun, or even a relative pronoun if a subordinate clause is to follow: /māta lwaladu lkabīru/ 'the big boy died', /māta llad̲īna qataltu-hum/ 'the ones whom I killed (them) died'. Independent personal pronominal subjects of verbs are rare and introduced only for emphasis. The subject must be in the nominative, and must, if it is a phrase, be endocentric—that is, it must include at least one word, usually in the initial position, which could stand alone as subject. If a stated subject follows the verb, the verb agrees with it only in gender, whereas all subsequent verbs, pronouns, or adjectives referring to it must agree in gender and number; if, however, no subject is stated, the sentence may begin with a plural verb, and all subsequent agreement will be with the implied subject: /qatala rrijālu/ 'the men killed' vs. /qatalūn killed' vs. /qatalū/ 'they killed'. (In this context it is worth repeating that normally the plurals of all words not referring to rational beings are grammatically feminine singular.)

(c) The remaining constituents of the clause, if they are nouns or endocentric noun phrases, must be in the accusative; however, there may be a clause or a particle standing alone or introducing a clause or a noun phrase. Direct objects precede adverbials: /kataba lwaladu lmaktūba lyawma/ 'the boy wrote the letter today' has verb-subject-object-adverbial /dāma lwaladu karīman/ 'the boy remained noble', /dāma lwaladu bi-lbayti/ 'the boy remained in the house', and /dāma lwaladu yaktubu/ 'the boy continued to write', provide examples of an accusative complement, a phrase introduced by a particle, and a clause consisting of a single imperfect verb.

Arabic also has a type of clause without any verb. These clauses have the order:

$$+ \text{ subject } + \text{ complement } \pm \text{ adverbial(s)}$$

The positions of complement and adverbial may be filled by the same forms as those listed under (c) above, except that the complement, if it is an endocentric noun phrase, must be nominative. The subject, like the subject of a verbal clause, must be endocentric; however, nominal clauses are much more likely to have pronominal subjects, and their subjects may be accusative if they are introduced by certain particles.

Nominal clauses are frequently translated into English with the present tense of the verb 'to be': /lwaladu fī-lbayti lyawma/ 'the boy is in the house today', /baytu-hu kabīrun/ 'his house is big'.

In the simplest case, where the complement is an indefinite noun (including most adjectives in this position) or is not nominal and the subject is definite, there is no difficulty in dividing the sentence. However, where both are definite: */rrajulu lmaliku/ 'the man is the king'; or indefinite: */mulūkun kirāmun/ 'kings are generous', a third person pronoun may be interposed as a copula: /rrajulu huwa lmaliku/ 'the man, he is the king'; or a particle may be set before the subject which makes it accusative: /ˀinna rrajula lmaliku/ 'indeed, the man is the king'. Such particles are very frequent, and are often necessary for some other aspect of the meaning. Where the subject is indefinite and the complement is prepositional, many such clauses translate English 'there is' and are then reversed: /bi-lbayti waladun/ 'there is a boy in the house', or /εindī maktūbun/ 'I have a letter' (lit., 'there is a letter with me').

Subordinate clauses may be introduced at a number of different points, and many would be accounted for by a fuller discussion of the particles, which would have to deal with the problem of interpreting the tense of the verb in the subordinate clause in relation to that of the main clause. Two types are worth special notice:

(a) The *ḥāl* ('circumstantial') clause: The position of circumstantial complement may be filled by a clause usually introduced by /wa-/ 'and', which here acts as a subordinating particle (sometimes accompanied by other markers, especially /qad/ for the perfect), translated 'while, when, although, but,' etc., which requires that the tense of the verb it governs be interpreted in relation to the main clause: /kataba maktūban wahuwa malikun/ 'he wrote a letter while (or although) he was king'; /sayastaqbilunī waqad qaraʾa maktūbī/ 'he will receive me now that he has read my letter'.

(b) The relative clause: this must always contain a pronominal reference to the noun it modifies in the main clause, but there is no relative pronoun if the noun modified is indefinite: /kataba maktūbayni qabiltu-humā/ 'he wrote two letters which I received'; /kataba rajulun māta lyawma maktūban/ 'a man who died today wrote a letter' (lit., 'he wrote - a man - he died today - a letter'). If the relative clause refers to a definite noun, that noun is followed by a relative pronoun agreeing with it in number and gender: /kataba rrajulu lladī māta lyawma maktūban/ 'the man who died today wrote a letter'. The relative is a member of the main clause, from which it takes its case, and may stand alone: /kataba lladī māta.../ 'the one who died wrote...'

1.73 *Major types of noun phrases*

In endocentric noun phrases, the member of the phrase that could stand alone usually stands first and shows the case that fits its role in the sentence. It may be modified by another noun acting as an adjective which agrees with it grammatically in number, gender, and definiteness: /lbaytu lkabīru/ 'the big house', /kātibatun karīmatun/ 'a noble secretary (fem.)', /bi-bayti-hi lkabīri/ 'in his large house'. It may be followed by a genitive determining complement in the *iḍāfa* ('construct'): the first member of a construct phrase cannot have nunation or the definite article and is generally determined by the following noun, so that any subsequent adjective modifying it directly must be definite: /baytu lkātibati ikabīru/ 'the large house of the secretary (fem.)'. Occasionally, if the second member is indefinite, the first may be treated as indefinite: /maktūbu rajulin/ may be 'the letter of a man' or 'a letter of a man'. Construct phrases are treated like words—they have only a single marker of determination (on the last member) and a single marker of their role in the sentence (on the first); thus, they may be in construct to still another noun, and adjectives modifying any member of the construct phrase must follow. Constructs express more than possession, as the following examples show: /karīmu nnafsi/ 'noble of soul', /ʔakbaru madīnatin/ 'greatest of cities', /qabla lḥarbi/ 'before the war'. A construct modifying a definite noun may have an initial definite article: /lmaliku lkarīmu nnafsi/ 'the king noble of soul'.

1.74 *The role of the case and modal endings*

On the basis of the previous discussion, it is clear that the loss of final short vowels in all dialects of Arabic, and the fact that these are not indicated in the writing and are only pronounced in context forms (see 1.24), must be considered in relation to their relatively minor importance in Classical Arabic. It has hardly been necessary to discuss the use of the modes, since these are mainly marked by specific particles and the vast majority of unmarked verbs are indicative. Among the nouns, the fact that determination is indicated only on the second member of the construct and that the word order in the phrase is not variable is generally sufficient to mark this type of phrase, while all other genitives are associated with prepositions. So long as the order described above is maintained, there is little difficulty in distinguishing functions marked by the nominative and genitive case. Writers of Classical Arabic differ in the extent to which they deviate from this order and exploit stylistically the flexibility of word order which is present in theory. Many stylistic devices which make it possible to stress some element besides the verb may be analyzed in terms of the word order described here, particularly the use of a nominal sentence with a clause as its complement: /ˀinna lmalikata māta ṣadīquhā/ 'indeed, the queen [is a person who] her friend died' (instead of /māta ṣadīqu l-malikati/ 'the queen's friend died').

NOTES

1. Charles A. Ferguson, 'The Emphatic ḻ in Arabic', *Language* 32.446-52 (1956).
2. Joseph H. Greenberg, 'The Patterning of Root Morphemes in Semitic', *Word* 6.162–81 (1950).
3. Henri Fleisch, S.J., L'Arabe classique: *Esquisse d'une structure linguistique* (Beirut, 1956), from which Table 2 is adapted.

2. THE HISTORY OF CLASSICAL ARABIC

2.1 The Semitic family of languages

Arabic is a member of a family of languages which have been spoken for millennia in areas where Arabic is now in use or in immediately adjacent areas. These languages are called Semitic languages and their interarelationship is evident from similarities of structure which make it possible to reconstruct a parent language, Proto-Semitic, from which they are all descended. Semitic languages still in use are, besides Arabic: Ethiopic, especially as Amharic, the modern language of Ethiopia; the South Arabic languages, a group of languages including Mehrī and Soqotrī, spoken by a small population in the south of Arabia; Hebrew, the language of the state of Israel, which had fallen from use as a spoken language for over two thousand years until its revival by the Zionists; Aramaic, spoken in a cluster of villages in the Anti-Lebanon north of Damascus, and its near relation, Syriac, spoken by groups in Iran and Iraq. Arabic (sometimes called Northern Arabic for greater clarity) is by far the most important Semitic language, with over eighty million speakers.

Arabic, Ethiopic, and the South Arabic languages are especially closely related, forming a cluster or sub-grouping known as South (or Southwest) Semitic, and our knowledge of them is comparatively recent. In contrast, Akkadian, the long-dead language of the Assyrian and early Babylonian Empires, is known from approximately 2500 B.C.; with the various forms and regional dialects it developed before it died out completely about A.D. 100, Akkadian is considered to be a separate, Eastern branch of Semitic, set apart from the Western branches by a highly deviant verbal inflection, a simplified phonology, and the use of š̠ in a number of morphological positions where other Semitic languages have *h* ~ ʾ.

The remaining Semitic languages have usually been classed as the Western or Northwestern group: the Canaanite dialects, including Hebrew, the languages of a number of other peoples mentioned in the Old Testament, and Phoenician, which was an important commercial language, later the language of Carthage, form one branch; and Aramaic, the language spoken in Palestine at the time of Christ and the later administrative language of Babylon (the Eastern branch of Aramaic is called Syriac) forms the other.

These are quite rough groupings and there is considerable dispute about the precise relationships between these languages and groups of languages. The first inscriptions in West Semitic only go back to 1400 B.C., so it is hard to specify its relationship to Akkadian, although reconstructions of older fragments of a language called Amorite provide some hints of a link. Ugaritic, written in cuneiform on clay tablets which were discovered at Ras Shamra in 1929, has stimulated new discussions of the relationships within West Semitic. There is, however, no doubt of the general pattern of relationships, as all of these languages are characterized by a series of consonants corresponding to the emphatic and emphatic-like consonants of Arabic and a morphology based on triliteral consonant roots interlocking with derivational patterns. Semitic itself is a member of the Hamito-Semitic (Afro-Asiatic) superfamily, which includes Egyptian (from Ancient Egyptian to Coptic), Libico-Berber, and the Cushitic languages. Here the precise relationships are even more difficult to determine.

Among the Semitic languages, Arabic is conspicuous as showing the features that characterize Semitic in a very fully realized form—that is to say, it has a rich inventory of consonants and a highly elaborated system of derivation from the triliteral root. Semiticists differ on whether this was true of Proto-Semitic and has been blurred in the other Semitic languages, or whether the system was originally much more rudimentary and has in Arabic simply been pushed, by analogy, towards its logical conclusion. This seems to be the case, for example, of the derived verbs. Akkadian has four forms (primary, geminate causative with š equivalent to Arabic /ˀa-/ in Form IV, and passive with *n*); each of these may have infixed *t*, *tan*, or *tata* (although the last, especially, is very rare). By including fossilized forms, it can be shown that Ethiopic has a very symmetrical system in which each one of the three forms produced without affixes (*qatala*, *qattala*, and *qātala*) appears alone and with each possible affix (e.g. *qatala* yields *qatala, aqtala, astaqtala,* and *taqatla*; and so on for the three others). Since Arabic also has a number of rare forms that were omitted in the preceding structural sketch, any attempt to postulate a system for Proto-Semitic which exploits all the derivational devices surviving in the attested languages results in almost twenty types. This is probably a case where, starting from a system which included a tendency toward this type of derivation, the different languages have produced different analogous elaborations. Classical Arabic is the only language with a full set of passives made by vowel alternation and has a very complex system, while the Northwest Semitic languages have quite simple ones. The case seems to be much the same with the pronouns, since the same components appear in all of them, with the same gender distinctions (in the demonstratives, for example, *d̲* (~[z]) for the singular, *t* for the feminine and *l* for the plural), but the forms are variously augmented, and the partial use of vowels to distinguish gender varies greatly. In Ethiopic, the use of *-k* in second person pronominal suffixes has been extended to the agent suffixes of verbs, e.g. *qatalka*, second person masculine singular perfect.

Arabic phonology is very close to the reconstructed phonology of Proto-Semitic. Proto-Semitic **p* > Arabic /f/ and Proto-Semitic **g* > Arabic /j/, which patterns as the voiced consonant corresponding to /š/ instead of /k/, causing some realignment in the system. The complicated system of Proto-Semitic sibilants is shuffled, and Arabic /s/ represents the merger of two different Proto-Semitic phonemes. In contrast to this, all the other Semitic languages except Ugaritic have lost a number of phonemes, especially the interdentals and the consonants formed toward the back of the mouth (e.g. in Akkadian, Proto-Semitic *ʾ, **g*, **ḥ*, *ε, and **h* as well as **y* and **w* are all realized as ʾ). The Arabic vowel system, with three vowel positions and phonemic length, seems to preserve the original system, but colloquial dialects share the trend of other Semitic languages to develop phonemic stress and increase the number of vowels.

In general, features of Arabic grammar which are notably conservative have often been lost in the colloquials, which have in many cases developed in directions attested in earlier forms of other Semitic languages. One area in which a degree of complexity retained in Arabic has often been lost elsewhere is inflection for number; the dual especially has tended to be limited to a few frozen forms, just as dual verbal and pronominal forms have tended to disappear in the colloquial. Furthermore, although modern Classical Arabic stands somewhere between an aspect system and a tense system, this evolution has been completed in a number of Semitic languages and in some colloquial forms of Arabic, often with the generalization of the active participle as a present tense. In the same way, the loss of final short vowels and nunation (mimation, with *m* instead of *n*, in other Semitic languages), which characterizes the shift from Classical to Colloquial Arabic, occurred much earlier in other offshoots of Semitic.

2.2 The Arabic writing system

Unlike some of the related languages (Egyptian, attested by hieroglyphs from 3000 B.C., and Akkadian, first attested in 2400 B.C.), the earliest clearly Arabic inscriptions are dated as A.D. 512 and 568, and there is no abundance of written records until well into the Islamic period. The peoples of Arabia had first contacted writing as it was used in the Mediterranean empires, primarily for Aramaic. At an early period, the speakers of South Arabic in the Sabaean kingdom of Yemen adopted one of the early Canaanite alphabets for their own use, with twenty-nine letters without ligatures. Inscriptions in this orthography have been found in various parts of Arabia (Liḥyānic, Thamūdic, and Ṣafāitic), and it now serves, after a number of radical changes, as the writing system of Ethiopia. Speakers of Arabic began to use the Aramaic alphabet (with forms very like those of modern Hebrew) as early as the beginning of the Christian era, but they wrote in Aramaic. This usage developed in two Arab kingdoms which had brief periods of power, the Nabatean kingdom at Petra, which was conquered by Rome in 106, and Palmyra, conquered in 273, but the so-called Sinaitic inscriptions were being made by Nabateans until as late as A.D. 300. Over the years, more and more Arabic forms from the spoken language filtered into writing, and a certain number of ligatures begin to appear between the slowly simplified forms of the letters. The modern Arabic script is descended from this Nabatean script, which was subjected to a number of modifications to suit the phonology of Arabic.

The Nabatean alphabet fell short of meeting the needs of Arabic in a number of ways. First of all, Arabic has a number of consonants which do not occur in Aramaic: /ṯ/, /ḏ/, /ḥ/, /ġ/, /ẓ/, and /ḍ/. Second, the simplification of the letter forms and the introduction of ligatures to form a cursive script had resulted in the loss of a number of distinctions which had existed previously; for instance, a small tooth or wiggle in the line of script had to represent the consonants /b/, /t/, /n/, and /y/, as well as the Arabic phoneme /ṯ/ (because of its similarity to /t/). For some positions in the word, the Arabic alphabet had only fifteen letter shapes to represent twenty-eight consonant phonemes. This made reading extremely difficult, and various solutions were experimented with even before the rise of Islam in the seventh century A.D. The oldest written records in Islam—coins from the middle of the seventh century, inscriptions on tombs and milestones soon after, and papyruses by the end of that century—show that dots were already beginning to be placed above or below the letters, in groups of one, two, or three, to distinguish identically written consonants. The system was not completely worked out for another hundred years: dots were used sporadically and inconsistently and some of the conventions used at the time (for /f/ and /q/) were later changed. From about the middle of the eighth century on, however, the use of the dots as necessary and regular parts of the letters was stabilized and the undotted script was only used for decorative inscriptions.

Like other Semitic alphabets, however, the adapted Nabatean used by the Arabs is purely consonantal. This is appropriate to the structure of the Semitic languages, where most of the meaning is lodged in the consonantal skeleton of the word, particularly in the root, and the vowels can usually be deduced; in fact, transcriptions of Arabic, such as that used in the present study, tend to blur the basic structure of grammatical forms. When long vowels were analyzed as short vowel plus semivowel, as they eventually were in the more evolved forms of most Semitic alphabets, the semivowel was written, with the result that parts of the consonantal structure which had tended to be lost in the earliest orthography were restored and a number of important grammatical distinctions made possible. In the modern Arabic alphabet, the letters *wāw* and *yāˀ* (/w/ and /y/) are used to indicate /ū/ and /ī/, and /aw/ and /ay/ as well, and the *alif* (or occasionally *yāˀ* in final position) to indicate /ā/. *Alif* is also used to indicate prosthetic syllables, and some word divisions. Since *alif* had originally represented a phoneme (the glottal stop /ˀ/), a new sign had to be invented for this, and after some experimentation the grammarians settled on a sign called *hamza*, a small version of the initial form of the letter *εayn* (/ε/). This sign was integrated into the sequence of letters by being set on one of them as a support. *Alif* is the most frequent support, but later *wāw* and *yāˀ* were pressed into service if the glottal stop was followed or preceded by /u/ or /i/. Choosing a support for *hamza* is complicated, but once chosen it gives some information about the short vowel environment. At about the same time, a miniature /š/ called *shadda* was adopted to stand over doubled consonants. Although the *hamza* and *shadda* are not consistently indicated, they are considered part of the script and are written in the same ink as the basic letter forms.

Arabic is written from right to left in a graceful, highly cursive script. All the letters may be attached to a preceding letter but there are six which are never joined to a following letter. Many of the letters have special forms after a space, they are at their simplest when connected left and right, and most of the letters are provided with loops at the end of the word. The positional variation in letter shapes indicates word separation, and there is nothing equivalent to our system of capitalization. These elements, with the additional strokes which three letters require for their basic shape, make up the cursive line of Arabic.

However appropriate the consonantal system was, a study of the preceding grammatical sketch will show that there are many instances of ambiguities which can only be resolved by specifying the short vowels. Even before the invention of *hamza* and *shadda*, the Arabs experimented with the use of dots for short vowels—placed above a consonant followed by /a/, in the letter for /u/, and below it for /i/. These were distinguished from the consonantal dots by the use of colored inks, usually red, while the cursive line was written in black. The use of red ink for vowel marking, along with the association of the position with particular vowels, continued after the adoption of new vowel signs (attributed to the grammarian al-Khalīl) which were small, simplified versions of the letters *alif, wāw*, and *yāʾ*. These are doubled to indicate nunation. This system was in use by the middle of the eighth century for the Qur'ān, where accuracy was vital. Its use is still limited to the Qur'ān, poetry, children's books, and occasional helpful hints at points where confusion is very likely. The vowels are not indicated in the normal printing of books and newspapers or in medieval prose manuscripts.

Arabs are very conscious of the beauties of calligraphy and have developed a number of decorative scripts (especially *Kūfī* and *Thuluth*); the frequent use of writing for decoration is partly linked to the prohibition on pictorial representation. Arabs write between, rather than on the lines, and achieve a straight left margin and other aesthetic balance by the extreme lengthening of some letter forms. Commentaries, or even totally separate books, are often written in the margins. The commonest of the scripts which were developed for use on papyrus is called *naskhī* and is now used for most Arabic printing; this hand is frequently taught to Westerners, although most Arabs east of Tripolitania use the so-called *ruqεa* script for handwriting, a simplified script developed for chancellory use. Various scripts are used for printing and handwriting in North Africa; /f/ and /q/ are dotted somewhat differently, and Sudanese writing is considered thick and clumsy, while Algerian is unusually angular.

The Arab conquests and the spread of Islam caused the spread of Arabic and of the Arabic alphabet. Almost all Muslim peoples have used the alphabet at some time or other; in addition to Arabic, it has been used for Persian (and other Iranian languages), Osmanli, the Turkish of Turkey (and other Turkic languages, including Uighur and Kazakh), Urdu, and Malay. In Africa it has been used for Berber (except by the Tuaregs), Swahili, Hausa, dialects in the area of Lake Chad, and occasional others. Osmanli, Malay, and all Turkic in use in Communist China have adapted Latin alphabets, while the Arabic alphabet has been replaced in the Soviet Union, after experiments with various Latin alphabets, by modified Cyrillic. Iran and Pakistan are the two most important non-Arabic-speaking countries using the Arabic script today, and both of these use a script called *nestaεlīq* (often called *taεlīq* in the West). *Nestaεlīq* is a jagged script, heavily influenced by the old Pahlevi (an early form of Persian) orthography; the word slopes down towards the end (the left), with long-drawn-out final loops. Because it is more difficult to print, it is being replaced by *naskhī* in Pakistani use, beginning with the newspapers.

The system of dots was extended to distinguish consonants which occur in these other languages ([p], [č], [g], etc.) and these are now occasionally used in Arabic for unassimilated loanwords. Arabic consonant letters which did not reflect phonemic differences in the borrowing languages were generally retained in words borrowed from Arabic. The consonantal alphabet of Arabic is not appropriate to the Turkic and Indo-European languages that have used it; it tends to make reading difficult and to favor the readily recognizable Arabic loanwords. Turkish, which has a complicated system of vowels and vowel harmony, used the symbols for the emphatic consonants to indicate the presence of back vowels, but this was a makeshift and imperfect technique.

2.3 Arabic literature

2.31 *Pre-Islamic literature and the Qur'ān*

The history of Arabic literature begins in the sixth century with the highly institutionalized uses of poetry in the tribal society of Arabia. Since then, Arabic has been first the language of a vast Islamic empire, then one of many Islamic languages, retaining its special privileges only in areas directly related to religion, and finally the language of a number of nation states entering the modern world and responding to its aesthetics as well as to its technology and political ideology. The need to keep Classical

Arabic, as the vehicle of the religious tradition, as 'pure' as possible was in constant tension with the struggle to adapt this language, which was probably never in general use, to new didactic and expressive aims. Both of these pressures have tended to reinforce a stress on form rather than content which began in the pre-Islamic period.

In the century before Islam, poetic forms were already highly developed, and the role of the poet was an important one. His poetry was public and on his eloquence depended the honor of the tribe and the mockery of their enemies. In the most elaborate form of composition, the *qaṣīda* ('ode'), the poet would follow a stylized sequence of themes, establishing his poetic authority by his skill in describing the traces left at an abandoned encampment and his nostalgia for some romance that took place there, followed by a journey or description of his horse or camel, reflecting his own valor. After this preparation, he would conclude the poem with a political or a personal statement, often a panegyric. A number of metrical forms, based on the alternation of long and short syllables, were available to him, and the same rhyme had to be maintained on all the fifty to a hundred lines of the poem. A similar form, but without the rigid sequence of themes, was used for elegies, and a non-metrical rhymed prose, *sajε*, seems to have been used by soothsayers and for proverbs.

These forms seem to represent the main uses of the poetic language in formal, intertribal communication, and they possessed the authority, always very high for the Arabs, of eloquence. When Muḥammad began the revelation of the Qur'ān in A.D. 610, a process which continued until his death in 632, he was compared to both poets and soothsayers, who were believed to be possessed by demons, and had to defend the special divinely inspired nature of his words even as he was slowly finding new resources of style for the expression of novel ideas. Because he was accused of being a poet, he spoke very harshly of poetry in general. The early *sūras* (chapters) are very lyrical, quite short, and contain elements of both poetry and *sajε*, but the later ones, composed when Muḥammad was governing and legislating for the city of Medina, to which he had fled in 622

(A. H. 1, the first year of the Muslim era), are the earliest evidence we have of Arabic prose, and were probably cast in a style developed by Muḥammad himself, although the stylistic development has been obscured by the arbitrary arrangement of *sūras* in the canonical form of the Qur'ān.

Subsequently, a large proportion of Arabic literary effort was to be devoted to the interpretation of the Qur'ān, making use of pre-Islamic poetry as linguistic evidence, but there were great differences in composition and preservation between the two forms.

The odes seem to have been composed by professional poets who, although capable of improvising, would often labor long over a poem and generally composed the passages dealing with single themes as unified wholes, memorizing them themselves or reciting them to professional reciters, who were often 'apprentice poets', who would commit them to memory section by section for public recitation. This oral tradition maintained considerable linguistic homogeneity within a standard 'poetic language' and preserved lengthy poems for two centuries and more. Muḥammad, on the other hand, had had no such apprenticeship, so that his use of the poetic language is tinged by the local usage of the Quraysh tribe of Mecca. Supposedly, he recited sections of the Book just as he received them from the Archangel Gabriel, with little or no polishing. In this case, the memorization was done by a number of people or fragmentary passages were recorded on whatever writing materials were available, which were then transmitted back and forth between the Companions of the Prophet, each trying to expand the portion of the text he knew by heart and supplementing it by a developing tradition of exchanging accounts of the Prophet's words or doings (*ḥadīth*). The practice of memorizing the Qur'ān is still a common one, but in the warfare that accompanied the spread of Islam too many of the Companions were being killed and the first Caliph (successor to the Prophet), Abū Bakr, had a complete manuscript prepared in 633, which was revised under the Caliph εUthmān in 651 and put into its final form. Since the early Arabic script did not indicate vowels, oral tradition was still necessary to determine readings of the Qur'ān, often making a great difference of meaning. This left a loophole for dispute and uncertainty which was not closed until the reign of εAbd al-Malik (685–705) when the diacritical marks were introduced, reflecting a reading of the Qur'ān which shows a slight normalization of Qurayshite usage.

2.32 *Umayyad literature*

During the first four 'orthodox' caliphates and under the Umayyad dynasty of caliphs who ruled the empire from Damascus from 661 to 750, literary production was small. Poetry survived Muḥammad's disapproval and continued in the pre-Islamic tradition except for a shift in values and a tendency to break down the ode into more occasional pieces (love songs, wine songs). In Syria, three rival poets, al-Akhṭal, al-Farazdaq, and Jarīr, abused each other in verse, skillfully and often obscenely. In Mecca, which had become a very gay city under the impact of the pilgrimages and the revenue they brought, poetry, especially love poetry, was set to music, while in Medina, a much soberer city, in which the Muslim sciences were beginning to develop, a parallel tradition of love poetry developed; instead of the gay poems of coquetry and seduction written by εUmar b. Abī Rabīεa at Mecca, Medina produced near epics of disappointed love. Meanwhile, an oral tradition, especially in the garrison cities of Iraq, dealt with accumulated teachings about the life of the Prophet and the best interpretation of the Book. A great part of the literary production of the εAbbāsid dynasty which followed consisted of the writing down of materials which had crystallized in spoken form in the previous era and the collection of pre-Islamic poetry which was still memorized and recited in town and desert.

2.33 *εAbbāsid literature*

2.331 *The Islamic sciences*

The εAbbāsid dynasty was established in 750. The εAbbāsids based their power on Islam, rather than identifying with the

Arabs, and moved their capital to Baghdad, where they were enriched by the creativity of Persian converts to Islam. The dynasty flourished for about a hundred years (the famous reign of Hārūn al-Rashīd (786–809) falls in this period), and then came to lean more and more on Praetorian guards of slave-soldiers. Local governments became increasingly autonomous, and there was a long period of decline. The Classical Age of Arabic literature, which began under the εAbbāsids and continued under other local dynasties, ends with the sack of Baghdad by the Mongols in 1258. During the εAbbāsid period, literature was tremendously stimulated by the generous patronage of a court which was fully alive to its possibilities for entertainment and its utility in the search for clear and final formulations on points of religious controversy and in the induction of new converts into Islamic and Arabic civilization. Translations from Persian and from Greek, via Syriac, provided an additional stimulus, and the establishment of a paper factory in Baghdad in 795 made it possible to write and own many books and to transfer the oral tradition to written form.

The need for clarification of religious questions led to the development of the Muslim sciences of Qur'ānic exegesis, law, and tradition (*ḥadīth*). Qur'ānic exegesis depended on a knowledge of Arabic grammar, which was being investigated at Baṣra and Kūfa, the garrison cities of Iraq. In these new cities, scholars who were often of Persian origin gathered linguistic data by collecting the ancient poetry and by questioning Bedouins, who were thought to speak a purer form of Arabic. The main collections of poetry were written down between 750 and 900, and a number of anthologies were put together. One of the most famous of these, *al-Muεallaqāt*, included one poem each by seven of the foremost pre-Islamic poets: Imru'u l-Qays (famous for a long section describing amorous intrigues, and for the description of a storm with which it closes), Ṭarafa (with at least forty lines of description of his camel), Zuhayr (preaching against war), Labīd, εAntara, εAmr b. Kulthūm, and Ḥārith b. Ḥilliza. Other anthologies included shorter poems as well as complete odes, and two of the most famous, which were arranged by topics, bear the same title, *Ḥamāsa* [Fortitude], for their first and longest section. These were compiled by Abū Tammām (d. 850), himself a poet, and al-Buḥturī (d. 897). While some philologists became so fascinated by the study of the ancient poetry that this became a separate branch of learning, others were formulating the rules of Arabic grammar, culminating in the great work of Sibawayh, called simply *al-Kitāb* [The Book].

The study of history also developed to meet religious needs. The mass of lore about the life and sayings of the Prophet, each anecdote being supported by a chain of authority by which it had ostensibly been passed on from the Companions of the Prophet, was used as a source of doctrine. When heterodox tendencies developed in Islam, traditions supporting all sorts of contradictory dogmas were attributed to Muḥammad and the chains of authority (*isnād*) forged, so that a science of *ḥadīth* developed to identify them. Six collections of traditions were eventually accepted as genuine (*ṣaḥīḥ*), of which the first two by al-Bukhārī (d. 870) and Muslim (d. 874) are the most important. Traditions relating to Muḥammad's life had been woven into a continuous narrative (the *Sīra*) by Ibn Isḥāq in the eighth century (written down in the ninth), stories of the conquest (*maghāzī*) were collected at the same time, and the type of reference work (*ṭabaqāt* 'categories') which was to become so common in Islam, with entries on long lists of scholars, poets, etc., was invented by Ibn Saεd (d. 845) when he wrote *Kitābu l-ṭabaqāti l-kabīr* classifying all the Companions of the Prophet with their lives and genealogies and criteria for determining the authenticity of *ḥadīth*. By the time of al-Ṭabarī (d. 922) history was established as a separate science, and it was possible for this scholar to write a commentary on the Qur'ān, which served as the basis for most later exegesis, and a universal history to illuminate the revelation of God's purpose through world events. *The History of Prophets and Kings* of al-Ṭabarī is written much like a collection of traditions: each fact or point of view is supported by a chain of authority, and several versions of the same event are set side by side, without being integrated in a continuous narrative, beginning with the creation of the world and concentrating on the history of the Islamic empire. History continued to be a major concern of Arabic literature, but although later works are mines of information about particular provinces or dynasties, no historian as interesting as al-Ṭabarī appeared until the fourteenth century.

2.332 *Belles lettres*

Another literary genre, known as *adab* ('belles lettres'), developed for those audiences, especially those around the court, that were concerned with combining edification with amusement and with obtaining enough information on any subject to appear educated. Such writings were especially useful to the class of secretaries and bureaucrats, primarily of non-Arab origin, who needed induction into Islamic civilization and models on which to base their style. *Adab* stemmed from a concern with philology, with increasing elaboration of the background material necessary for literacy, and finally came to range from pure entertainment to popularizations of difficult subjects, covering a spectrum about as wide as that which appears in the pages of today's *New Yorker* magazine, and often acted as the medium in which the tension between Arabism and the ethnic consciousness (*shuεūbīya*) of the non-Arab converts was expressed.

On the purely entertainment side, although often with morals attached, we find the Arabic version of the Sanskrit *Fables of Bidpai*, composed by εAbdullāh b. al-Muqaffaε (d. 760), and the *Arabian Nights*, various versions of which crystallized from Sanskrit and Persian models in the tenth century. Another common style was the stringing together of instruction and anecdote, as in the *Book of Animals* by al-Jāḥiẓ (d. 869), *The Unique Necklace*, composed in Spain by Ibn εAbdi Rabbihi (d. 940), and the *Book of Songs* by Abū l-Faraj al-Isfahānī (d. 967), which uses a collection of Arabian poems set to music as the basis for an eclectic discussion of the incidents which occasioned their composition, the lives of the poets and their patrons, and the conditions of life in pre-Islamic Arabia. More edifying popularizations were written by Ibn Qutayba (d. 889), and some of his titles, set among works on history and literary criticism, state the nature of this type of belles lettres very explicitly: *The Fountains of Story, The Book of Subjects of Knowledge, The Adab of the Secretary* (here often translated 'culture' or 'accomplishments'). This tradition was carried into the eleventh century by Abū l-Ḥayyān al-

Tawḥīdī (d. 1023) and al-Thaεālibī (d. 1038). The secretaries themselves developed a stylistic tradition, using rhymed prose with highly self-conscious elaboration, in their letters (*risāla*, pl. *rasā'il*) especially those of Ibn al-Amīd (d. 970), al-Khawārizmī (d. 993) and al-Ṣāḥib (d. 995).

The last really important stylistic innovation of Classical Arabic prose was the *maqāma* (often translated 'assembly'), created by Badīεu l-Zamān al-Ḥamadānī (d. 1007), and then developed by al-Ḥarīrī to one of the liveliest branches of Arabic literature. In the *maqāmāt* a series of vignettes are strung together, describing in rhymed prose, with every possible rhetorical device, the encounters of the narrator with a lovable ruffian who recounts his exploits. During the modern period, the *maqāma* has had almost as great a prestige as the *qaṣīda*, and just as modern poetry was to struggle with the effort to modernize or abandon the qaṣīda, the *maqāma* was felt to have the authority of a native Arabic literary form which might be developed into drama or into an Arab novel.

Poetry had always been the Arab art *par excellence* and was invaded by non-Arabs with much greater trepidation, since the philologists who had collected and studied the ancient poetry had rigidly defined the nature of poetics and the permissible subjects and styles, comparing each new work with the ancient models. The sphere of prose, however, was constantly expanded, so that poetry lost its position as the only medium with rhetorical authority; according to one tradition, prose supplanted poetry in the middle of the ninth century. Nevertheless, poetry was an essential part of court life, and it is possible to follow several tendencies in its development. There was an increasing specialization, with a greater development of love songs and wine songs (Abū Nuwās (d. 810), one of the greatest of Arabic poets, a famous member of the court of Hārūn al-Rashīd who appears in the Arabian Nights), or ascetic and *ṣūfī* (mystic) verse (Abū l-εAtāhiya (d. 828)). New metaphorical devices, called *badīε* ('innovation'), enriched all poetry, even that which remained close to the classical tradition, but was carried to extreme lengths in a branch of poetry that was decidedly un-Arab in feeling. *Badīε* was invented by Bashshār b. Burd (d. 783), a blind poet of Persian origin, and was adopted by a series of poets, al-Sanawbarī, Kushājim, and εUqaylī, who created ever more elaborate tropes describing wine and garden landscapes. This poetry of refinement was in strong contrast with a slangy form of poetry which was developing in the great towns of Mesopotamia. However, two of the most distinguished poets of the period, al-Mutanabbī and Abū Firās (d. 968), both of whom lived at the glittering court of Sayfu l-Dawla in Aleppo, preferred to go back to the classical tradition, and a later poet, known for his free-thinking and the tortuous elaboration of his prose, al-Maεarrī (d. 1057), followed their precedent from a linguistic point of view.

2.34 *Arabic literature in decline*

Towards the end of the εAbbāsid period and in the centuries that followed, Arabic literature lost most of its vigor, lasting slightly longer in Spain than in the East. Poetry was the earliest genre to decline, for although there were always scores of poets ready to copy the old forms, the only creative voices were those of the *ṣūfis* and mystics who used poetry to express their religious experiences, εUmar b. al-Fārīḍ(d. 1235) and Ibn εArabī (d. 1240). The *adab* tradition was already languishing in the eleventh century and al-Ḥarīrī was the last great innovator in that tradition. More serious forms of prose writing lasted longer: *ṭaabaqāt* of importance continued to be written (for instance, the *Biographical Dictionary* of Ibn Khallikān, (d. 1282), and the work of encyclopedists such as al-Suyūṭī (d. 1505)). A North African, Ibn Khaldūn (1332–1406), propounded a magnificent theory of history which is explained in his *Muqaddima*, based on the group cohesiveness which gives the nomads their advantage in a cyclic struggle with dynasties following an internal law of decay. However, he lived at a time when originality was a rare exception.

Philosophy was one of the later forms of classical literature to develop in Arabic, beginning with al-Kindī (d. 850) and al-Farābī (d. 950), and continuing with Ibn Sinā [Avicenna] (d. 1037), al-Ghazālī (d. 1111) the great reconciler of ṣūfism and orthodoxy, and Ibn Rushd [Averroës] (d. 1198), but it could not survive the religious rigidity of the years that followed. Geography, which was initiated by Ibn Khurdādbih, in charge of εAbbāsid posts in the ninth century, had a rich development during which it absorbed many of the features of *adab*, as the wonders of foreign lands became more intriguing than the details of desert life, and reached a high point in the travels of Ibn Baṭṭūṭa (d. 1377).

Although Arabic literature had started its decline two centuries before the Mongol sack of Baghdad in 1258, the effect of the sack itself was not as drastic as might have been expected, because the Islamic world had already long ceased to be centralized around a single imperial capital. During the long years of disintegration, two areas that had been of immense importance to Arabic literature were completely eliminated as possible sources: Spain, when the Moors were first oppressed and then driven out, and Persia, as the Persian language replaced Arabic and Persians began to glorify their own pre-Islamic past. From the end of the fifteenth century to the beginning of the modern period, the Arab lands were ruled from Istanbul by Ottoman Turks, and these centuries were almost completely unproductive, partly due to decay and misrule, but also in great part to the fact that membership in the ruling class was open to those who learned Turkish and became Ottomans, so that talent from all over the empire was attracted to this new imperial identity. Arabic was no longer the only language of Islam, and the use of Arabic no longer conferred prestige and was required only in some specifically religious contexts where the concern was with continuity and memorization, rather than with creativity. The story of Arabic literature stops here and does not resume until the nineteenth century, when the new literature begins to be Arab as well as Arabic.

2.35 *Modern Arabic literature*

The modern period opened for the Arabs in 1798 when Napoleon landed in Egypt, although it took another fifty years before a new Arab literature really began to take shape for the Arab Renaissance (*nahḍa*)[1]. The first steps were the efforts of Muḥammad εAlī and his followers who ruled Egypt after the

French withdrawal and who had seen enough of modern Western methods to want to train technicians in the new skills, either by sending them to Europe or by establishing schools in Egypt. The next generation, the children of these technicians, became intellectuals trying to define first the political-philosophical and then the aesthetic canons of the new era, and they were supplemented by a steady stream of Syrians and Lebanese, many of whom had been trained in Christian missionary schools established in the second half of the nineteenth century.

Nineteenth century Arabic literature was composed of several strands. The first was woven by journalists and essayists commenting on day-to-day problems and putting them in an ideological setting. Al-Afghānī (d. 1897) and Muḥammad εAbduh (d. 1905) are the most famous thinkers of the period who tried to formulate, modernize, and purify Islam, while Muṣṭafā Kāmil (d. 1908) and Luṭfī al-Sayyid (d. 1963) were for creating a secular Western state. A great deal of translating was also done, both technical and literary, and drama was introduced to Arabic via translations and early experiments in dramatic rhymed prose by the Lebanese Naqqāsh family. At the same time, explicitly literary Arabic was still closely bound to the classical tradition: while the essayists strained at the limits of the *risāla*, these were much less confining than those of the *maqāma* and the *qaṣīda*, which were not replaced by novel and drama or by newer poetic forms until the beginning of the twentieth century. In poetry the *qaṣīda*, which has a considerable grip to this day, was the only area in which neoclassicism really flourished, in the work of such poets as the Egyptians al-Bārūdī (d. 1904), Aḥmad Shawqī (d. 1932), Ḥāfiẓ Ibrāhīm (d. 1932), εAlī al-Jārim (d. 1949), and εAzīz Abāẓa, or the Iraqi Maεrūf al-Ruṣāfī (d. 1945). These men varied in the strictness with which they conformed to the classical model, sometimes using the standard content of Bedouin poetry, with desert camp sites and camels, and sometimes interpreting the sequence of themes more abstractly, for instance, transposing the journey theme to a modern vehicle, but they all used the metrical forms and the lexical elaboration that characterized the classical ode.

In the first quarter of the twentieth century, a generation of

Arab writers appeared in Egypt who were much more clearly in favor of westernization and secularization than the previous generation, and relied on an underlying national character, which they visualized as going back to the Pharaohs, to preserve a fundamentally Egyptian flavor in their writing. Many of these writers are still living; they include Muḥammad Ḥusayn Haykal, who wrote the first truly Arabic novels, introducing colloquial Arabic for dialogue; Ṭāha Ḥusayn, perhaps the most famous of modern Egyptian writers, who was also at one time minister of education, and whose autobiography *The Days* has been translated into several western languages; εAbbās Maḥmūd al-εAqqād and εAbd al-Qādir al-Māzinī (d. 1949), journalist-essayists; Tawfīq al-Ḥakīm and Maḥmūd Taymūr, who created the modern Arabic drama; and finally Aḥmad Amīn, who set out out to write a vast social and intellectual history of Islam. During this period, some of the poets who were later to carry their rebellion much further published collections of verse where, without undertaking a real rupture with tradition, they endeavored to loosen its hold, and eliminate the archaisms that made neoclassical poetry stiff and artificial. The Lebanese Muṭrān Khalīl Mutrān and the Egyptian εAbd al-Raḥmān Shukrī published such collections in 1908 and 1909 respectively, still as very young men.

This period of working towards a lucid modernism ended in the twenties[2], and perhaps its bankruptcy should be dated at the publication in 1926 of Ṭāha Ḥusayn's famous book on pre-Islamic poetry in which he outraged orthodoxy by suggesting that the whole corpus of pre-Islamic poetry had been forged under Islam by the reciters and philologists, so that, by implication, all Qur'ānic interpretations based on its linguistic evidence were invalid. The reaction to this suggestion was so vehement that the book was withdrawn and later reissued with offensive passages removed. The response to the discovery of the superficial relationship between these westernizing writers and the society they lived in was not an attempt to return to Classical norms, but a surge of emotionalism and subjectivity in literature and a tendency towards reaction and xenophobia in political thought. Ten years earlier, εAbd al-Raḥmān Shukrī had published for a few brief years in a strain of exaltant, romantic self-discovery, and now this strand was picked up in the poetry of *wijdān* ('emotion'), which supplanted the enlightened neoclassicism. The poets of *wijdān* tended to be essayists as well, highly conscious of themselves as investigating the nature of poetic truth, especially εAbbās Maḥmūd al-εAqqād, εAbd al-Qādir al-Māzinī, Ibrāhīm Nājī (d. 1953), and Abū l-Qāsim al-Shābbī (d. 1934). Although it was short-lived, the journal *Apollo*, published in Cairo from 1932 to 1934 and almost completely written by Aḥmad Zakī Abū Shādī, was a pivotal influence in the search for 'pure poetry' and the abandonment of all the classical prosodic forms.

After World War II, Beirut became increasingly important as a literary and intellectual center. This was partly due to the fact that the work of emigré writers, the writers of the *Mahjar* in America, who were able, living outside the Arab world, to make radical experiments in form while continuing to write in Arabic, had begun to be reabsorbed. Lebanese writers of importance include Faraḥ Anṭūn, Amīn al-Rayḥānī (d. 1940), Mīkhā'īl Nuεayma, Muṭrān Khalīl Muṭrān and Jubrān Khalīl Jubrān. This last poet is well known for his English writings as well, where his name takes the form Khalil Gibran (*The Prophet*, etc.), and the prose poem which he used so effectively became, with free verse, one of the vehicles used by this generation.

By the late fifties and early sixties, Arabic literature began to lose this quality of revolution and counter-revolution. Older writers are conscious of how far their positions have moved, while younger ones see the old battle lines as blurred and are more concerned with expressing themselves as individuals and experimenting with types of symbolism rather than with linguistic forms, since the predominance of free verse exemplifies the consummation of formal experimentation. The linguistic problems that remain are those faced by the whole community, namely, the fact that however far experiments with written Arabic are taken, it is still not the normal spoken language of any part of the Arab world. Contemporary essayists have developed a mature style and contemporary poets find obscurities of thought as attractive as obscurities of diction were once burdensome. The greatest problems are faced by novelists and dramatists who must make the formal idiom as natural and true to life as they can, and they must work this out in relation to television, radio, and moving pictures, which are becoming more and more important. However, the modern Arab novel, in the hands of such writers as Suhayl Idrīs of Lebanon and Najīb Maḥfūẓ of Egypt, has by now come of age.

There are many young Arabs writing now in all the Arab countries so that it is not possible to point to a single center or to list half a dozen names. Two important trends can be mentioned in addition to the trend towards symbolism described above: the appearance of a number of important women writers (Nāzik al-Malā'ika, an Iraqi poetess, and Layla Baεalbakī, a Lebanese novelist, author of *I Live*, are two examples), and the increase in short stories, many of them describing the life of villagers or slum dwellers. Arabic has come to be a language in which the role of the writer and the different literary genres open to him are quite closely comparable to the literary roles and genres of European literature. No longer is he a tribal functionary, no longer is his every use of the language interwoven with the religious-philological tradition, or made the means of inducting non-Arabs into a civilization. Arabs write today as individuals with greater or lesser degrees of religious or social engagement, essentially seeking their own best self-expression in the next best thing to a mother tongue. The fact that the language they write is not their mother tongue is part of a complex situation which will be described in Chapter 3.

2.4 The influence of Arabic on other languages

Before discussing the actual use of Classical Arabic in the Arab lands today, it is necessary to give some indication of the influence of Arabic on a number of other languages in areas where Classical Arabic is not now the standard written language.

The areas where Arabic triumphed were primarily those where some form of Semitic was already in use; the interaction of Arabic with these other forms is part of the problem of the colloquials, and will be dealt with in the next chapter. In areas where non-Semitic languages were in use (especially Berber in North Africa, Indo-Iranian in Persia and India, and Turkic in Asia

Minor, the Caucasus, and Central Asia), the original languages survived, but the conversion of their speakers to Islam had drastic effects. Arabic is one of the major languages of civilization, like Latin or Chinese, with a pervasive effect in the areas of its influence throughout the Islamic world. This effect was linked to the fact that the linguistic style of the Qur'ān and Muḥammad's use of Arabic were considered necessary and intrinsic parts of revelation, so that the Qur'ān could not, in orthodox Islam, be translated, read, or recited in any other language. To this day, pious Muslims from Indonesia to the Sahara know lengthy portions of Arabic by heart although they may have no active control of the language, may drastically distort the phonology, and have a varying comprehension of what they are saying. Furthermore, the technical vocabulary of the new religion, some of it Qur'ānic and some of it coined to describe increasing institutionalization, entered the lexicon of the converted peoples. Since Islam influences every sphere of life and law, this has meant that vast numbers of Arabic loanwords entered other languages, including most of the words referring to the apparatus of government.

The adoption of the Arabic alphabet, because it was so much more appropriate to Arabic morphological forms, tended to reinforce these borrowings, both by making them easier to read and by dramatizing the relationships between words derived from the same root. As usual with linguistic borrowing, the vast majority of the loans were noun forms but these included verbal nouns and participles from the derived forms, so that the recognition of roots was important. A number of particles were also borrowed.

In addition, it is clear from an examination of the figures who created Arabic literature that during the period when Islam was united, a knowledge of Arabic was necessary for any scholarly or political advancement—Arabic was an imperial language—and ambitious and talented men of all national backgrounds used Arabic as their medium for all kinds of written expression. Those who could not write pure Arabic did their best and those who could not really write Arabic at all wrote their own languages with as many Arabic loans as possible. When Arabic ceased to be the imperial language, nations with an old tradition of civilization, especially Persia, used their own languages except when dealing with specifically religious subjects, but the vast number of loanwords and the alphabet that fostered them were retained. Nations Islamized after the decline of the caliphate often looked to Persia as a center of civilization, but in borrowing from Persia they took at least as much Arabic as Persian. Up to the nineteenth century, it was virtually possible, with a knowledge of Arabic and the Arabic alphabet, to read Ottoman Turkish, Persian, and Urdu. Writers in these languages included the whole lexicon of Arabic for possible use and treated most Arabic forms according to the grammatical rules of their source.

Modern nationalistic movements and the decline in religious and classical education have affected these loans to varying degrees. The Turks of modern Turkey have abandoned the Arabic alphabet of Ottoman, do not teach Arabic in the schools, and have made a conscious effort to purge the language of Arabic and Persian loans. Urdu in Pakistan and Persian in Iran are still written in the old alphabet and still show many loans, but the borrowings are no longer free and even these Islamic languages have less and less in common. In areas of Africa where Islam is still spreading, Arabic moves with it as a language of civilization, and the old process tends to be partially repeated.

NOTES

1. I am indebted for much of this analysis of the modern period to the unpublished thesis of Jaroslav Stetkewycz, *Modern Arabic Poetic and Prose Language* (Harvard Univ., 1963).
2. Nadav Safran, *Egypt in Search of Political Community: An Analysis of the Intellectual and Political Evolution of Egypt, 1804–1952* (Harvard University Press, 1961) p. 165.

3. THE LINGUISTIC PRACTICE OF THE ARABS

3.1 Speech and writing in Classical Arabic

The preceding chapter has dealt with Arabic in relation to the other Semitic languages and with the external development of Arabic as a literary language up to the present, and the complex influences that it has had on the languages with which it has been in contact. The discussion so far has been an idealized history of only one of many dialects of Arabic, the one called εArabīya, omitting the development of the other dialects, the extent of their actual use, and the effect of these dialects and of other languages on the εArabīya. εArabīya is the Arabic term for what European writers call Classical, Written, or Literary Arabic; these terms are sometimes used in a more specialized way, whereby Classical Arabic refers to the language of the pre-Islamic poets (also called the poetic koine), Literary Arabic refers to the prose language of medieval Islam, and the modern uses are referred to as Modern Standard Arabic.

3.11 *The origins of Classical Arabic*

Pre-Islamic Arabia, like present-day Saudi Arabia, included pockets of urban and oasis settlement, often relatively prosperous stops on trade routes, and vast areas whose only population was nomadic. Communications were poor and there was no central administration, but at the same time there was a continual slow shuffling of population, with some degree of communication maintained over long periods of time and great distances. In this situation there was much dialect variation, although it is difficult to mark the boundaries of any particular dialect. The Arab grammarians recognized these dialect variations, referring to them to explain unusual forms and generally classifying them to reflect the tribal rivalries of their own period. Two large groupings of dialects have been identified[1]: the Western group, spoken in the mountainous strip that parallels the western coast of Arabia and the relatively fertile land lying between it and the coast and in another area on the Persian Gulf, and the Eastern group spoken in the remainder of the peninsula (except in those areas where South Arabic, a distinct language, was spoken; see 2.1). Western Arabic was spoken in Yemen and in the Ḥijāz, the area where Islam developed in the Holy Cities of Mecca and Medina. Eastern Arabic was the language of the important tribes of Tamīm, Rabīεa, Asad, and others of the Qays confederation, and was the dominant strain, in spite of heavy Western influences, in the Najd (the central area of the peninsula, to the northeast of the Ḥijāz); significantly, this is the area where the major experiments in political organization, the evanescent empire of Kinda and the Qays confederation, took place, and where Arabic poetry is said to have evolved (Imru'u_1-Qays, for instance, was a hereditary prince of Kinda). εArabīya or Classical Arabic seems to have developed in the Najd, combining features of several different dialects into a common language which was used for some kinds of intertribal communication. Phonologically, it resembles the Western dialects, which had a full vowel system, relatively little consonant assimilation, and two phonemes corresponding to /ā/ which are reflected in the two ways of spelling final /ā/ in ClA. On the other hand, the *hamza* /ˀ/ tended to be lost in the Western dialects, whereas the Eastern dialects preserved it, sometimes exaggerating it to /ε/; ClA preserves the *hamza* and resembles the Eastern dialects grammatically, so that it is probable that ClA is primarily Eastern, but that it developed quite early, before the most drastic phonetic alterations had occurred in the Eastern dialects. On the other hand, many of the Old Arabic inscriptions seem to be predominantly Western, and are certainly not direct ancestors of ClA. Western Arabic is of special interest because many of its grammatical features identify it as a link with Northwest Semitic.

Classical Arabic was associated with a particular type of poetry and was spread along with that poetic tradition to all parts of Arabia; it seems never to have been identical with any normal spoken dialect, so that it was necessary for poets to be trained in its use, but of course it was much more different from the dialects of Mecca and Medina than it was from the dialects of the Najd where it developed. Illiterate Bedouin tribes do not now use this dialect for poetic composition, but they do seem to have used it for several centuries after Islam, so that they remained useful informants for the philologists, and it is still true that in many areas oral poetry is composed in a different dialect from the dialect of normal speech, borrowing from a nearby or more Bedouin group or preserving archaic features[2]. It was associated with solemn or eloquent speech and was useful currency for intertribal communication, so it is not surprising that it was the appropriate medium for the Qur'ān. The various traditions of recitation and anomalous orthographic features of the Qur'ān remain a valuable source of information about Western Arabic.

The use of the poetic dialect, which is often referred to as a poetic koine (by analogy with Greek) because of its intertribal character, was reinforced as the Islamic community became increasingly mixed, commanding a supertribal loyalty. Although early writers seem to reflect a knowledge of the dialectal mixture in Arabia and the fact that the idiom of the Qur'ān was not that of the Quraysh tribe to which the Prophet belonged, Muslims of later centuries came to believe that the εArabīya was the normal speech of nomadic Arabia, that it had reached its fullest perfection in Quraysh, and that all deviations from it were corruptions. As the result of the labors of the philologists, the poetic dialect was codified to the point where it became a much more homogeneous language than it had ever been in the mouths of the pre-Islamic poets. The grammatical rules reflect a knowledge of a standard separate from the Qur'ān, and the original mixture of dialects is reflected in the great lexical richness of Classical Arabic.

3.12 *Classical Arabic in the Islamic Empire*

Classical Arabic must really be considered to date from the moment when the Islamic administration and the maintenance of religious orthodoxy put a premium on the use of a single, standardized, and unifying dialect. Classical Arabic represents the ancient poetic koine frozen at a particular moment of its existence, whereas it must once have been relatively fluid—such a fluid state is reflected in the *dīwān*, or tribal anthology, of the Hudhayl tribe, collected in the early Islamic period, which shows considerable deviation from the Classical norm. Even more deviant forms, of which Muḥammad's own is one example (although most of these have tended to be normalized wherever they were written down), must have been used by those who were not professional poets, but took advantage of the inter-tribal dialect for trade and politics. Within less than a century, the love poetry written in the Ḥijāz (see 2.32) reflected radical changes in style and some linguistic change, which can only partly be attributed to non-Arab elements of the population.

Nevertheless, a real effort was made to maintain Classical Arabic as the language of the court[3]. This was always a self-conscious process, which included a great deal of discussion of the correct forms, and was made possible by continually drawing on Bedouins, especially *rāwīs*, the professional reciters of poetry who were trained in the poetic koine, and by sending young men to visit in Bedouin tribes. 'Puristic' anecdotes date from the end of the seventh century. It seems to have been extremely difficult, however, to maintain this dual tradition and by the ninth century almost no effort was made to use *iεrāb* ('Bedouin' speech with full inflectional endings) in conversation. The standard of mastery of Classical Arabic seems to have steadily declined, lasting only slightly longer in the centers of culture and administration than it did in the tribal areas, until it became the preserve of experts—the grammarians who made a lifelong study of it and trained their own students to carry on their traditions. The lapse of Classical Arabic from spoken use probably corresponds quite closely to the point where it became fully a written language—where illiterates no longer mastered it and the norm was set by written style to which formal speech might make an effort to conform. As the Arab empire declined, first Persian and then Turkish edged Classical Arabic out of more and more areas of use and forced it to become more and more specialized.

A comparison with the preceding chapter will show that the great body of Arabic literature was produced after the spoken use of the language began to decline and that much of it was addressed to just this problem. The procedure was a cumbersome one, however; there was never a very large group of men with sufficient training to produce literature, and during a period of massive cultural decline the rigors of training in Classical Arabic tended to limit it to pedants and its use to specifically religious scholarship.

3.13 *The modern use of Classical Arabic*

Whereas during the pre-Islamic period the spoken dialects were primarily tribal, they became regional and now have an increasing tendency to be national. Classical Arabic has always had a number of special contexts which demanded its use, has required some degree of special training in a language different from the language of childhood and family life which was only acquired by a portion of the population, and has carried with it prestige and access to the richest portions of the culture. The modern Arab world represents a continuation of this situation, which has been called *diglossia*[4]. The other face of diglossia, namely the nature and distribution of the vernaculars, will be explored below (see 3.2).

Classical Arabic in its secular use is now an international language; in the modern Middle East, it is the language which Iraq, Syria, Jordan, Egypt, Lebanon, Tunisia, Libya, the Sudan, Morocco, Algeria, Saudi Arabia, Yemen, Kuwait, Aden, etc., have in common. It has been adopted by all of these countries as an official language and is the only form of Arabic which achieves full official recognition. Its importance goes even further than this, for it is the chief symbol of ethnic unity among the Arabs and is essential to any kind of Pan-Arabism. Any attempt to resolve the problems of diglossia by moving towards a more extensive use of the regional dialects runs into the impassioned opposition of those who see ClA as the essential basis for the common Arab nation; an Arab is defined as anyone who 'speaks Arabic and thinks of himself as an Arab', and this is a definition which is only meaningful if it is taken, ideally, as referring to ClA, since the regional dialects are not all mutually intelligible. Arabs who cannot use ClA to some degree may have to fall back on English or French (if they know these languages; see 3.3) if they come from widely separated regions. Therefore, ClA still possesses that vital element which was the basis for its adoption as the language of the Islamic *umma* ('community'): it is a unifying factor, nowadays crossing the borders of different political systems, different economic environments, widely varying cultures and physical types, and different religions. It is also international in the sense that it is the form of Arabic which is most used in international contact with non-Arab nations: the BBC transmits broadcasts in ClA and international treaties and agreements with Arab nations have versions in ClA.

Classical Arabic is also international in its religious and liturgical use and in religious courts as the language of Islam. The Qur'ān may be discussed in colloquial or in other Muslim languages like Urdu, but it is normally read in ClA. Translations have generally been regarded as invalid and limited to marginal groups like the Ahmadīya and the Black Muslims in the United States, and this may well remain true for Islam as an international religion. In this context, the εArabīya embraces an even wider sphere and becomes of paramount value to theologians who cherish the unity of Islam.

Classical Arabic still retains the connotation which it had as a poetic koine of being more beautiful and more significant—indeed, this is often carried to the point where the elegant expression of an idea may be taken as evidence of its validity. ClA is the language in which important things are said, in addressing God, in crossing national boundaries, and in science and the arts. The same emphasis on form that is so apparent in the historical development of Arabic literature has its counterpart today in a lingering tendency to judge what is said by the way in which it is said. Furthermore, many Arabs take pleasure in listening to ClA even when they are unable to understand the content and may write long passages of eloquent double-talk for the pleasure of the language, which are read with little awareness that the information conveyed is minimal. The inflectional grammar of the written language is regarded as a work of art, whereas Arabs are often unwilling to recognize that the dialects have any grammar, but see them as chaotic deviations from the sacred norm. Educated Arabs feel very strongly about grammatical correctness and will almost always find fault with a passage they are asked to correct—and often, too, when they are not asked. The feeling that Arabic grammar embodies a high and difficult truth is expressed in a general scepticism about the possibility of any non-Arab ever 'really' learning Arabic. This may be very discouraging to students, especially if they do not realize that the modern educated Arab, unless he is a specialist, is himself far from being at home in Classical poetry and prose, and is very often at a loss for the correct inflectional form. Since ClA is the only form of the language which is normally written, it is pragmatically the only way of access (except for European languages) to any form of education or culture or to any participation in the national life outside the local scene. All books and newspapers are in Classical Arabic, all translations from European languages are into ClA, and all formal instruction is in ClA. Most radio broadcasting is in the classical language, as are almost all political speeches. All correspondence takes place in the only form of Arabic that can be written and in theory all bureaucratic functions depend on it.

It is worth pointing out that in most of these contexts the level of correctness achieved may be quite low. Radio broadcasts may be understood by those who could not begin to approximate them, and most Arabs, when they are dealing with printed material, do not maintain an awareness of the grammatical functions which would be necessary in order to read it out loud correctly—they seem to read the consonantal skeleton and to get enough information from it to understand the grammatical construction without being able to achieve a full vocalization. They may write the same way, and it is a feature of modern Arabic style that it is relatively hospitable to this approach. Furthermore, while Classical Arabic is used in formal instruction and prepared lectures, discussion slips readily into modified forms of Colloquial. Similarly, government officials may discuss written material which is in front of them in Colloquial. However, all this takes place in contexts where the initial tone is set and the basic material provided by the written language, so that although academic and intellectual subjects may be discussed in the dialects,

ClA provides the framework for the discussion, and participation is hardly possible for the fully illiterate. A model for this may be found in dealing with literature written in the dialects: in many parts of the Arab world aside from the use of passages of colloquial dialogue, songs and folklore have been collected in dialect and conventions adopted for writing these in the Arabic alphabet. However, these written forms of Colloquial Arabic are normally used only by those who have arrived at literacy via the classical language itself.

In the modern renaissance, the sphere of Classical Arabic has been greatly expanded, not so much because of a change in the nature of the situation of diglossia, but because the new spheres of life in which Arabic is used in the twentieth century tend to fall into the categories governed by Classical: the use of the radio and the introduction of drama fall in this category, and so does most advertising and propaganda. Furthermore, the importance of science is radically increased and ClA has been stretched to accommodate new concepts and vocabularies (see 3.142), just as it has been challenged to meet new art forms. This is in contrast to the relatively more stable nature of the areas of colloquial expression in rural areas and in family and other informal conversation. Much of the terminology which deals with political and technological conditions is borrowed into Colloquial either from Classical or from European languages, with Classical playing the more important role. What this means is that the confrontation with the twentieth century has tended to take place in ClA because it is international, because it is 'eloquent' and 'significant', and because it is written. Not only is it the Arab's only entry to his cultural resources in the past and in other parts of the Arab world, it is his primary entry into the future.

Unfortunately; the medieval situation is still reflected in the fact that ClA remains the possession of an elite. All of the Arab countries are engaged, to varying degrees, in fighting illiteracy, since the spread of the ability to read is not only practically necessary for the smooth functioning of a modern society, but has a heavy ideological load. Those who cannot read are in many ways disinherited, and in the Arab countries they face special obstacles because they must acquire a new language in order to learn.

This leads to the suggestion that the only way of 'democratizing' Arabic is to write the vernaculars in a modernized script, so that literacy will depend simply on the mastery of a rational script for writing the generally spoken language; in the Soviet Union, for instance, several modified Cyrillic alphabets have been developed for writing the Arabic dialects spoken by groups of Arabic speakers in Central Asia (the residue of the furthest wave of conquests), effectively democratizing the language and at the same time fragmenting these groups and cutting them off from Arab nationalism and a share in the old and new cultural wealth of the Arab world.

Diglossia deepens the plight of the illiterate because it means that he may be unable to understand news broadcasts and political speeches along with his inability to grasp these in their written form. It also makes illiteracy much more difficult to combat and complicates primary education. Fifteen years ago, adult illiteracy (by even the most rudimentary definition of literacy) ranged between 85% and 90% throughout North Africa and in Iraq, went higher than 95% in Saudi Arabia and the other political units of the Arabian Peninsula, with slightly better rates in the Fertile Crescent: 70–75% in Jordan and 50–55% in Lebanon[5]. The rate was everywhere highest for women and in rural areas. Since that time, all of the countries have legislated universal, free elementary education through the sixth year, but none of the Arab countries has actually succeeded in registering all children (especially girls) in elementary schools; the programs usually omit nomadic population (as do literacy figures in the census), and are seriously deficient in rural areas. Programs to spread literacy among the adult population have been rather limited.

3.14 *The modern form of Classical Arabic*[6]

Although Classical Arabic has been extensively studied, focussing on the norms established by the grammarians or on the language of specific literature, especially the Qur'ān, Arabs and westerners have tended to assume that all written Arabic was essentially the same, reflecting various degrees of purity or affectation. This doctrine has been the basis of most teaching, and it is true that the structural sketch in Chapter 1 is applicable to all written Arabic, from the Qur'ān to tomorrow's newspapers in Cairo or Damascus. However, several important kinds of change are taking place which are leading to an extensive differentiation of 'Modern Standard Arabic'.

(1) There exist a series of 'acceptable' simplifications in realizing ClA, and there are a number of overlapping ways in which ClA is influenced by the dialects or accommodates to them.

(2) There is a vast shift in the lexicon, due to the need for technical terminology, which remains a critical problem in the Arab world; this sometimes has grammatical implications. In this context, the general nature of the Arabic lexicon may be summed up.

(3) There are a number of stylistic changes due to translations from European languages and extensive bilingualism.

These changes are, in general, due either to the spread of literacy or to the diffusion of European culture and seem to be signs of vitality in the language, which may or may not be able to unfold sufficiently rapidly to meet the need.

3.141 *Simplifications and Colloquial influences*

Most simplifications that are acceptable in writing are based on a limitation in the range of forms—the omission of syntactic structures used by classical authors and a drastic reduction in vocabulary. There is some tolerance for vagueness in, for instance, the exact reference of pronouns or the choice of the appropriate tense in conditional sentences. In general, modern written Arabic accommodates to the dialects by the selection of forms that are not dependent on short vowels for their understanding, whereas 'classicizing' and the search for a loftier style take place in the lexical range, sometimes by the selection, where ClA offers two forms, of the less colloquial, e.g. the use of /ḥīna/ 'when' instead of /lamma/, which also appears in the dialects. Many particles have undergone a slight shift in meaning /ḥattā/ 'until' often means 'even', and /ˀiḏā/ 'when' means 'if'. Particles play an increasingly important role in the sentence, defining tenses more precisely

(/sawfa/ + imperfect for the future), and expressing relationships which might be expressed by the construct (such constructions usually use the Classical /bi-/, /min/, etc., but in the Syrian area /tābiε/ 'according to, pertaining to' [ClA 'following'] is very common: /lajnatu lmuwāṣalāti ddāʾimatu ttābiεatu lilʾamānati lεāmmati lijāmiεati dduwali lεarabīyah/ 'the Permanent Commission on Communications of the Secretary General of the Arab League') and indicating indefiniteness: /baytun/ 'a house' > /ʾaḥadu lbuyūt/. One example of an analogical extension is the occasional use of /-ūn/ for adjectives modifying plurals of rational masculine beings, even where a broken plural exists, e.g. /kabīr/ 'big' appears with the plural /kabīrūn/ instead of /kibār/ by analogy with participles and adjectives with suffixed /-īy/. A few feminine superlatives are used simply as adjectives, appearing in both definite and indefinite: /šarikatun kubrā/ 'a big company'.

There is a further group of forms which are not reflected in the writing but are strictly errors in the pronunciation of ClA and yet are tolerated. Spoken ClA is sufficiently influenced by colloquial pronunciation and idiom so that it is almost always possible to tell where a broadcast originates; the Egyptian radio[7] (which is most notorious for this) maintains the [g] pronunciation of the Classical /j/ and follows the Colloquial stress patterns, since stress is generally a regional feature and not really part of the ClA system. ClA /ṯ/, /ḏ/, and /ẓ/ (=[ḏ̣]) have become dentals /t/, /d/, /ḍ/ in most urban dialects, and where speakers cannot produce interdentals, [s], [z], and [ẓ] are accepted. For all practical purposes, the number system described in 1.33 does not exist in the oral use of ClA—the short vowel patterns are a myth and the speaker uses the simplified forms current in his own dialect for numbers above ten, even though he may be able to write the correct consonantal skeleton. Most important, the ClA convention for omitting short vowel endings in pause (see 1.24) gives the Arab an escape route, for by breaking his sentence into shorter segments he may legitimately omit many of the grammatical endings which discomfit him. In slovenly speech which would not be acceptable on the radio, all forms may be in pause, except where the following word begins with a consonant cluster, especially in construct, and here a colorless vowel may be supplied. The contrast of pause vs. context has become much more flexible than it was and Arabs vary in their pronunciation of feminine nouns in pause (/-ah/, /-at/, or /-a/), of the adjective suffix (/-ī/ or /-īy/) and of indefinite masculine accusatives (traditionally /-ā/, now normally /-an/).

3.142 *Lexical development*

The historical Arabic lexicon includes vast numbers of words from different areas and epochs. Since all the accumulated nuances of these words have been preserved with them, meanings in context are often difficult to determine. When dictionaries of synonyms were written, words for 'camel' or 'sword', 'rain' or 'lion' stretched into long lists; side by side with these, dictionaries of special vocabulary dealt with the highly specialized terms developed in nomadic Arabia for plants or topographical features or points of the camel's anatomy. Every Arabic word is said to have four meanings: its primary meaning—the precise opposite—something obscene—something to do with a camel! In practice, only a small portion of this vast accumulated vocabulary is used, except for conscious and conspicuous archaism, and words listed in traditional dictionaries with half a dozen very different meanings are now generally limited to one or two. Outside of the portion in general use, the ancient vocabulary provides a treasury of words which may be analogically reinterpreted to fit modern contexts: two relatively rare words for caravan, /qitār/ and /say. yarāh/, are now in use for 'train' and 'automobile', respectively. Modern biologists sometimes reapply to specific forms of flora and fauna words whose precise ancient meanings are unknown.

Although the various linguistic academies in the Arab world sympathize with this technique, it is relatively cumbersome for purposeful use, because the fact that a word is already in existence in an obscure dictionary does not absolve modern users of the necessity of learning it in its modern definition and there is a certain amount of negative feedback. On the other hand, it is one of the chief methods of vocabulary development in a natural evolution. It has been especially important as Arabic has borrowed specialized usages of words which were originally Arabic but were borrowed by Persian and then Turkish; many modern administrative terms fall into this category.

The Arabic lexicon is structured by the various patterns for derivation of nouns and verbs from existing roots, and all dictionaries are organized around these roots. The relationship between meaning and pattern is, as has been pointed out, rather vague and subject to semantic shift over long periods of time, but where patterns are still open (e.g. muCāCaCah is still open to new coinages as a verbal noun for Form III verbs, whereas CiCāC, which sometimes occurs, is not; similarly, the derivation of quadriliteral roots by adding a fourth consonant between C_1 and C_3, the $^{ʔ}aC_1C_2aC_3{\sim}C_1aC_2C_3\bar{a}^{ʔ}$ adjectives for color and physical defects, and verbs of Forms IX and XI, and the others omitted in this treatment, are not) words may be coined quite freely, and if they are new coinages, there is some chance of guessing their meaning. Relatively few patterns are so open that they are freely innovated, but most patterns are available for the invention of technical terms:

Verbal nouns: /taˀmīn/ 'insurance', /taɛyīn/ 'ionization', /ˀiḏāɛah/ 'broadcasting'

Participles: /muˀtamar/ 'conference', /mantūjāt/ 'products'

Nouns of place: /maṣnaɛ/ 'factory', /mustašfā/ 'hospital', /maṭār/ 'airport'

It will be clear on consideration that these words represent a type of derivation which is radically different from that which occurs in Indo-European, especially in Latin and Greek, which are the reservoirs from which many European languages draw most of their technical vocabulary. First, because many technical terms are in part recognizable in English as such, e.g. we do not have to be told that 'television' means something more specific than the way the world looks from the top of a high hill; second, because English is one of a community of languages which share a technical vocabulary; and third, because (in very general terms) the Arabic system of derivation allows the Arab to combine only a single specific root, only one directly referential element, with a variety of modal specifications (gender, number, reference of the word to a place, a profession, a tool, a process, etc.). In coining a translation for 'television', Arabic would be constrained to choose between the reference to 'vision' and the reference to distance 'tele-'. The ideal system from the point of view of efficiency would (a) have a one-to-one correspondence, so the coinage could be automatic, and (b) would result in *single* words free to form syntactic combinations. These two features are virtually impossible to obtain without doing violence to the structure of Arabic.

In dealing with the suffixes and prefixes of Indo-European derivation, which do not have concrete references but have a semantic value (sub-, non-, semi-, post-; -like, -less, etc.) of the sort which generally occurs in particles in Arabic, the Arabs have tended to use their particles to form compounds which may only deviate from Arabic grammar when they are treated as unitary expressions—as words: /šibhu jazīrah/ 'peninsula', /ġayr qānūnīy/ 'illegal', /ḍidda jāsūsīyah/ 'counterespionage', /lā silkīyah/ 'wireless, radio'. These forms only show their strangeness in Arabic when they are used in context as single words, like the words they translate, but this procedure leads in turn to the treatment of Arabic phrases as single words as expressed in the addition of suffixes: /lā ʾadrī/ 'I don't know' becomes /lā ʾadrīyah/ 'agnosticism' or 'I don't know-ism'. Even this deviation from the spirit of the language is limited; 'semi-agnosticism' would be hard to express in a single word in Arabic!

ClA has also expanded the use of some of its modal affixes to translate technical terms, for instance the use of /-īyah/ to produce abstract nouns such as /marksīyah/ 'Marxism', /mašrūεīyah/ 'legitimacy', and /lā nihāʾīyah/ 'infinity'. Other modal affixes have been invented which, although they may be new, are not unlike existing morphemes. The chemist's suffixes *-ate* and *-ite* are simply taken over: /laban/ + /-āt/ → /labanāt/ 'lactate'; /kibrīt/ + /-īt/ → /kibrītīt/ 'sulfite'.

In the vast majority of cases, where translating requires two referential components, the attempt to produce a translation which preserves a one-to-one correspondence with the European technical term produces a phrase which cannot be used as a word: Noun + Adjective: /ḥukmun d̲ātīy/ 'autonomy'; Noun + Noun (in construct): /farṭu lḥāssīyah/ 'hypertension'; or, even more complex, Noun + Preposition + Noun: /qābilun lissuknah/ 'habitable, receptive to habitation'. On the other hand, the attempt to produce a single word does violence to the structure of the language, and such violence tends to be chaotic, so that many possible forms might result: /sarmanah/ from /ssayru fī lmanām/ 'going in sleep' and /nawmašah/ from /lmašyu fī nnawm/ 'walking in sleep' have both been coined for 'somnambulism'. Other examples of equal violence are /balmah/ 'dehydrate', a verb from /bilā māʾ/ 'without water', and /mutašājih/ 'isotope', an active participle from /tašābuhu jihan/ 'similarity of aspect', but these have the advantage that the violence has been done, in effect, at the root level, a process which is not without precedent (see 1.53), and they fit perfectly smoothly into the Arabic sentence[8]. It is in this category, where the choice is between a totally arbitrary translation (/raʾīs/ 'president' reflects only the meaning [or rather the use] but not the etymology or structure of the English word), the invention of a compound root, or the use of a phrase that will continually require recasting sentences, that the greatest lexical crisis exists, since the vast body of Western scientific terminology has this form, and all coinages of single words must be taught and cannot be recognized, while coinages of phrases are unstable.

To the reinterpretation and revival of old terms and the derivation of new ones by more or less orthodox means may be added a third source of new vocabulary, namely, direct borrowing from European languages. At all periods in its history, there have been borrowings into Arabic primarily from Indo-European and Semitic languages, and a number of loanwords have been recognized in the Qur'ān. Many Greek loans came into Arabic in the Middle Ages for the adaptation of the Greek sciences, and unlike earlier loans which fit relatively well into the Arabic phonological pattern (/ṣirāt/ 'path' from Latin *strata*), only a few of these could be fully assimilated (/falsaf/ 'philosophize') while the majority are painfully obvious (/jūġrāfīyah/ 'geography'). Such terms are somewhat difficult to manipulate in Arabic because only a few derivational processes can be applied to them, and it has been felt that they blemish Arabic style. In the modern period, nationalism has reinforced the resistance to such borrowings from European languages, and they tend to be regarded as a last resort. However, many words have been accepted completely and resist all efforts to replace them; /tilifūn/, for instance, has outlived more than a dozen suggested alternatives.

Modern borrowings from European languages include a number of Italian words, many English words (/kuktīl/, /faytāmīn/ and /fūlklūr/—note that this last is based on English spelling, not pronunciation), and the greatest influx of all, French words (/bitrūl/ 'petrol, gasoline'; /bilāj/ 'beach', Fr. *plage*, /lḥayātu lbūhīmīyah/ 'la vie de bohème', and /sīnamā/). Arabs are often urged, when adopting European terms derived from the Greek, to adopt a form based on the original Greek rather than its modern form, but this is often ignored. Arabs vary in the degree to which they pronounce loanwords in accordance with the phonology of the source language, and it is necessary to distinguish between European words used by Arabs in conversation, where both speakers may be bilingual, moving freely between the two languages and drawing on the second to fill any gaps in the first, and words which have been fully assimilated into Arabic, i.e. reshaped to an acceptable phonological form as reflected in a uniform spelling. Assimilated loans are very easily supplied with adjective endings (/sīnamāˀīy/ 'cinematic') and may be considered fully acclimatized when they are assigned a regular broken plural: /kakātīl/ 'cocktails', or /ˀaflām/, plural of /film/~/filim/.

3.143 *European influences on style and syntax*

In addition to the European influences that affect the lexicon, and which may be necessary for the development of a vocabulary for the discussion of modern life, European languages have also had a far-reaching effect on Arabic style because the modern Arab intellectual constantly moves back and forth between Arabic and French or English, and a great part of his Arabic reading is in translations, often carelessly and mechanically done. These influences are of two kinds: direct *calques* (component by component translations of phrases or idioms), and distributional changes, whereby constructions parallel or similar to those of French or English are favored, resulting in a slow shift of style.

Calques appear in such phrases as /lḥarbu lbāridah/ 'the cold war', /barīṭāniyā lɛuẓmā/ 'Great Britain', /qaṯala lwaqt/ 'kill time', /laɛiba dawran/ 'play a role', /ʔaxaḏa jiddīyan/ 'take seriously'. These are relatively obvious, but many others enter the language more subtly, appearing even in the works of stylists like Ṭaha Ḥusayn. Such calques are /qutila ɛalā yadi lfiransīyīn/ 'he was killed at the hand of the French', which not only includes a calqued idiom, but also the mention of the agent of a passive verb, which is normally forbidden by Arabic grammar; /kam huwa qarīb/ 'how close he is!' instead of the normal /mā ʔaqrabahu/, a special development of the elative; the use of /li-/ with verbs meaning 'to give' and /ʔilā/ with verbs of motion which take direct objects in literary Arabic; translation of 'there is, there are' by /hunāka/ or /hunālika/, which correctly only translate the 'there' in 'over there': /laysa hunāka ʔamalun fī.../ 'there is no hope that...' Even more subtle is the increasing frequency of such phrases as /ʔamwālu wamumtalakātu ššarikati/ 'the goods and properties of the company', instead of /ʔamwālu ššarikati wamumtalakātuhā/ 'the goods of the company and its properties', or /ʔusāʔilu nafsī/ 'I ask myself', instead of using a reflexive verb.

Distributional changes seem to result from the heavy volume of literal translations, which select among the available constructions of Arabic those constructions which parallel the original. The hack translator translates verbs into verbs and nouns into nouns, and in so doing he increases the ratio of nouns to verbs. He translates adverbs into adverbials, using the two available processes of ClA: accusative complements (/tadrījīyan/ 'gradually', /jiddīyan/ 'seriously') and prepositional phrases (/bittafṣīl/ 'in detail', /birifq/ 'tenderly'). He is continually involved in the effort to maintain the obligatory grammatical categories of the source language and so goes out of the way to specify time or nondetermination. He is repeatedly faced with phrases that have no perfect equivalent in Arabic, so he picks one which is approximately equivalent, and ends up using it so heavily that it is distorted (/ka-/ 'like' to translate English 'as', and a whole range of makeshift phrases to translate 'can', which is much commoner in English). Occasionally, he is so oppressed by the lack of a present of the verb 'to be' that he uses /maṯṯal/ 'represent'. And, above all, his work is scattered with such familiar phrases as /waṣaḥīḥan ʾan.../ 'it is true that...' or /yajibu ʾan yuḏkara ʾan.../ 'it must be pointed out that...'

Obviously, these features are most conspicuous in, for example, translations of news releases which must be available for immediate broadcast. Their effect may be very slight in the works of highly educated writers who are steeped in Arabic literature, so that it is difficult to appraise their over-all impact. It is generally true, however, that modern Arabic is becoming increasingly receptive to translation from Western languages, and this is probably a necessary evolution.

3.144 *Formal efforts at language reform*[9]

There have been a number of efforts to coordinate the vocabulary coinages of individuals and to control the modern developments in Arabic. The Egyptian Linguistic Academy, founded in 1922, was initially an independent organization of writers; it received official sanction in 1932 and continues today. Syria has had a Linguistic Academy since 1919, although it was somewhat eclipsed during the French occupation. Other Arab countries have followed suit with academies which encourage the publication of both classical and modern literature, 'pass' on suggested vocabulary coinages, propose new terms, and publish a journal to acquaint scholars with their activities. On the whole, the academies have not been very successful in their normative efforts, and much of the vocabulary they have sanctioned was never adopted. The development of separate academies in each country tended toward divisiveness, and in the thirties the academies began to try to coordinate their efforts, starting with the official language of treaties and the mails. Various professional groups have met to try and deal with their special lexical problems: physicians first in 1938, lawyers in 1944, engineers in 1946, and so on. In 1956 the academies held a general conference in Damascus and set up a coordinating committee to expedite their future work, all very much in the spirit of Arab nationalism;

a previous effort at coordination through the cultural committee of the Arab League, established in 1946, had not been a success.

The academies have also been faced with very sweeping proposals for reform: 'simplifications' of Arabic grammar, the adoption of colloquial Arabic for writing, orthographic reform. The most drastic proposals, including latinization, have been rejected, but the academies are much more sympathetic to attempts at simplification. There have been a number of promising efforts to simplify letter shapes so that they will vary less according to their position in the word, thus substantially reducing the cost of printing, and to provide for more information about the vowels.

3.2 Speech (and writing) in Colloquial Arabic

As far back as our knowledge and conjecture can reach, a multitude of other dialects have existed alongside Classical Arabic. The dialects have the obvious complementary characteristics to ClA: they are considered less elevated, they are general to the whole population (every Arab knows at least one as a first language), and they are regional and usually unwritten. They have further characteristics: it is difficult to set their precise boundaries, they are fluid over time, and they represent a more advanced stage of developmental trends which can be seen in other Semitic languages.

3.21 *The origins of Colloquial Arabic*

Because CoA is not normally written and the Arab grammarians were only interested in the dialects to the extent that these clarified odd constructions in ClA or as sources of error to be rooted out of literary usage, the origins of the particular dialects of CoA now in existence are not clear. Three types of hypothesis have been suggested: (a) that the modern dialects are degenerate forms of Classical Arabic, reflecting a gradual deterioration of usage which took place under the impact of the indigenous languages in the countries occupied by the Arab conquerors (this is the traditional Arab explanation, with slight variations); (b) that the present dialects are lineal descendants of pre-Islamic dialects spoken by the different tribes; (c) that they are descendants of some form of intertribal speech in use during the period of the conquests, containing a greater or lesser admixture of ClA, and owe their variation to the indigenous influences[10].

The second hypothesis is eliminated by an examination of the history of the conquests, since it is clear that in the original invasions Arabs from all parts of the peninsula were thrown together, and the division of the garrison cities into tribal quarters was a very fragile thing: even if we do not imagine the immediate homogenization of these groups, particular tribes emerged to dominate the situation in only a few areas. Furthermore, the dialects cannot be direct deteriorations of ClA since ClA was never generally spoken and the dialects contain a few features which seem to come directly from Semitic but do not appear in ClA. The modern dialects outside of Arabia (that is, in the areas conquered by the Arabs and colonized by them) seem to be descended from a form of Arabic which was neither identical to ClA nor homogeneous, but which included a whole range of dialect mixtures. Arab garrisons evidently developed a type of speech which included more or less similar proportions of influence from the different tribal areas, depended on the tradition of intertribal communication which had given rise to the poetic koine, and was subjected to strong influences both from the indigenous populations which rapidly adopted Arabic speech and the Classical language itself. The homogeneity of this form of speech was promoted by the movement of troops and individuals from place to place, a fluidity which continued to some degree right up to the decline of the εAbbāsid Empire, the Mongol and Turkic invasions, and the nomadization of vast areas, which drastically cut down on intercourse between urban centers and sedentary enclaves up to the modern period. The unity of this range of dialects also stems from the fact that they were all more innovative in the new linguistic environments, so that the internal developmental trends of Arabic moved more swiftly in all of these dialects than they had in nomadic Arabia or than they seem to have moved in the existing nomadic dialects. In contemporary discussions of Arabic dialectology, this range of dialects is referred to as the Arabic *koine*, which must be carefully distinguished from the poetic koine. The effort is made to deduce the features of this koine from the common features of the dialects descended from it, which have since diverged considerably. Such a hypothesis is not refuted by the demonstration that almost none of these features were completely common, since a reconstructed koine is more a demonstration of a general configuration than of a single uniform language believed to have been spoken at a particular point in time.

The Arab invaders of the first Islamic centuries, who must have spoken some form of this koine, merged with the local populations by intermarriage and by assimilating the outsiders as clients to their tribal groups, while these local populations (most of them Christian) became converted to Islam. Local varieties of the koine developed, and their speakers were almost completely sedentarized and became the ancestors of the city dwellers and villagers of the modern Middle East, the speakers of *sedentary* dialects. Members of later waves of migrations from the Arabian peninsula by tribal groups, many of which still remain nomadic or semi-nomadic, had not been involved in the formation of the koine but were somewhat more directly descended from the ancient dialects, and their descendants speak dialects which may be roughly characterized vis-à-vis the sedentary dialects as *nomadic* or *Bedouin*; the koine hypothesis is essentially an effort to deal with the sedentary-nomadic contrast, which is a striking one, although its dimensions vary somewhat from place to place. In the contemporary Middle East, it is no longer possible to say that all sedentary populations speak sedentary dialects and nomadic populations nomadic dialects, since many nomads have settled and some settled groups have been uprooted. The Arabs are often romantic about their nomadic past, regarding corruption as an inevitable result of urban life and looking to the Bedouin as more noble and virile', and, especially, as speaking a purer form of Arabic, so that where large groups of speakers of nomadic dialects have mixed with sedentary populations, the dialect has tended to become nomadized, the Muslims adopting nomadic features more quickly than the Christian and Jewish minorities. In modern

Baghdad, for instance, Muslims speak a nomadized dialect, while the minorities speak versions of a sedentary dialect which must originally have been spoken by the whole population. On the other hand, most of the nomadic invasions took place centuries ago, and there are regional characteristics cutting across sedentary-nomadic lines, so that it is possible to characterize *all* forms of Western Arabic vs. *all* forms of Eastern Arabic, or all forms of Mesopotamian Arabic vs. all other Eastern forms. Salient features of the dialects of the various large cities, which are of primary interest to the outsider, will be spelled out individually, but it is possible to state a series of developments which have taken place in all or nearly all forms of CoA, many of which can be recognized as part of the general developmental trend of Semitic, while others, occurring in the sedentary dialects, seem to point to a common origin in the hypothetical koine, especially when they are supplemented by a list of the contrasts between sedentary and nomadic dialects.

3.22 *General trends of development in Colloquial Arabic*

The most striking feature of CoA is that it has completely abandoned the system of nominal inflection for cases and verbal inflection for modes that existed in ClA by dropping all final short vowels. It is also generally more dependent on particles and word order than the classical language.

3.221 *Phonology*[11]

The points of the Classical system which were asymmetrical have been realigned in various ways. This realignment has affected the interdentals and the ancient emphatic lateralized dental fricative [ẓ$^{\lambda}$] which is transcribed in this handbook with its most common modern pronunciation, /ḍ/, but appears in the dialects in a number of different ways. The role of the palatals (/j/, /š/, /k/), and of the uvular /q/ has shifted. Emphasis has been extended to /l/ and /r/ and affects other phonemes near emphatics. Many short vowels (especially when unstressed, in open syllables, and more frequently /i/ and /u/) have been lost and long vowels shortened. Vowels have been affected by their contexts so that the old triangular vowel system has broken down. Diphthongs have been simplified to long vowels (/ay/ > /ē/ and /aw/ > /ō/) which sometimes have corresponding shorts; this has resulted in the development of a number of new syllable types (containing clusters excluded by ClA) and has been accompanied by the development of various sorts of stress.

By referring back to Sec. 1.2, it may be seen that these developments involve the loss of as many as four or five consonant phonemes (1.21) balanced by increased complexity of vowels (1.22) and syllable structure (1.23), while (1.24) the contrast of pause vs. context forms has been dropped, and stress has become more important (but variable from place to place).

3.222 *Morphology*

The loss of final short vowels (*iɛrāb*), sometimes referred to as the generalization of pause forms, accompanied by the generalization of the genitive-accusative forms of duals and sound masculine plurals, has been part of a general reduction in inflectional categories. Similarly, the dual has retrogressed in all of the dialects: it survives to some degree in the noun, but has disappeared from all pronominal or verbal forms, and dual nouns are treated, for the purpose of agreement, like animate plurals. The morphological processes described in 1.311 are all abandoned except determination by the definite article; this is complemented by an increase in syntactic complexity, including the frequent adoption of some form of indefinite article; residues of the pause-context contrast appear in the special forms which some nouns, especially feminine singulars and sound masculine plurals, take when they are in construct. (Residues of the accusative indefinite used adverbially are discussed under syntax.) The remaining categories of noun morphology and the system of nominal derivation are relatively stable, except that the number of noun types may be greatly reduced by the loss of short vowels (although aberrant types are often accepted), e.g. the loss of all unstressed short vowels in open syllables means that such contrasting sets as CaCāC—CiCāC—CuCāC or CaCūC—CuCūC are lost, and of course the functional specializations originally associated with these patterns tend to be blurred.

The Arabic number system (1.33) is everywhere radically simplified by the loss of *iɛrāb*; this simplification has been carried even further, however, in dialects outside of Arabia, and has striking common features in most of the Eastern sedentary dialects and in many Western ones: the anomalous handling of gender in ClA has been repatterned so that all counting is done with the old feminine forms (with no noun following) while enumerating is done with the old masculine forms, regardless of the gender of the following noun: Syr. /xamse/ 'five (the name of the number)' but /xams wlād/ 'five boys' and /xams banāt/ 'five girls' vs. ClA /xamsatu ʔawlād/ and /xamsu banāt/; residues of the ClA gender inversion remain in a number of special plurals used in enumerating which have an extraneous /t/: /xams tušhur/ 'five months', /xams tiyyām/ 'five days' vs. ClA /xamsatu ʔašhur/, /xamsatu ʔayyām/; furthermore, the '-teens' have been compounded into single words based on the ClA masculine: /xamsṭaɛš/ 'fifteen', with an emphatic /ṭ/, ClA /xamsata ɛašara/.

Verbal inflection (1.41) is simplified by the loss of all dual forms, while mode has ceased to be expressed by inflectional endings. However, almost all the dialects have introduced a prefix for the indicative (Syr. /birūḥ/ 'he goes' for the indicative, vs. /yrūḥ/ after a verb or particle expressing intention) and a number of ways of indicating tense more precisely, sometimes with a three-way system for past-present-future. The number of types of 'weak' verbs (1.413–15) are reduced in all dialects, but it is striking that these reductions, that is, the solution of a problem faced by all the dialects, were reached in a similar manner in most sedentary dialects (descended from the koine): C_3=/w/ verbs are treated exactly like the commoner C_3=/y/ (this is true of all derived verbs in ClA), while C_2=C_3 verbs are treated in the perfect like Form II final weak verbs: Syr. /maddēt/ 'I continued' (Form I) and /ṣaḷḷēt/ 'I prayed' (Form II) vs. ClA /madadtu/, /ṣallaytu/. In the area of verb derivation, the distinctions of the primary verb vowel patterns tend to be blurred, but the major derived forms survive, although sometimes only one or two examples of some forms can be discovered. The internal passive

(1.4221) has disappeared except in Saudi, again probably in relation to the decay of the short vowel system. The system of particles is expanded, and has an amplified importance, while the number of pronouns is reduced, parallel to the reduction in verb forms. In place of the ClA relative pronoun system, the dialects generally have only a single form.

3.223 *Syntax*

The major changes are directly related to morphological changes, as the language becomes increasingly synthetic and word order bears a heavier burden. CoA may have a more complex system of parts of speech than ClA as some dialects have developed an autonomous category of adverbs, many of them borrowed from ClA (Syr. /jiddan/ 'very', using the indefinite accusative ending). Phrase types, especially verbal phrases, are multiplied, and in many areas the typical sentence order is like that of English, where the subject precedes the verb.

3.224 *Lexicon*

The various dialects are always more hospitable to loanwords than ClA, but the primary source language varies from place to place (see 3.42). A conspicuous difference is that many varieties of CoA contain Turkish loanwords, which are extremely rare in ClA. Almost everywhere the doubly weak verb /raˀā/ 'see' has been replaced by /šāf yšūf/; the Classical /jāˀa bi-/ 'come with, bring' has been reshaped into /jāb yjīb/ 'bring'; and new forms have been adopted for 'what' (ClA /mā/, which had several different functions, now replaced by /ˀēš/, /šū/, etc.).

3.225 *Summary*

The loss of inflectional categories is the most obvious aspect of the ClA-CoA contrast, but equally important is the decline in importance of the almost algebraic root system of Classical due to (a) the increase in particles, which play a more important role as they carry the functions which were originally carried by inflection; (b) the loss or merger of derivational patterns so that word forms seem increasingly arbitrary; (c) the further separation of the semivowels from the consonantal system via the decay of diphthongs, the simplification of 'weak' verb inflection, and the shortening of final long vowels; (d) a general shift in the phonological shape of the word with a rise in assimilation and allophonic variation.

3.23 *Variation in Colloquial Arabic*

CoA varies in many different dimensions and has no single norm. In order to cover this wide range with some degree of efficiency, no single dialect will be fully described in the following sections, but certain fundamental features of groups of dialects may be inferred by interpreting the general trends of CoA in terms of (1) the nomadic-sedentary contrast and (2) the various geographical regions, with some specifics of the major prestige dialects.

3.231 *Contrasts between sedentary and nomadic dialects*

Just as the loss of case endings is the obvious point of contrast between ClA and CoA, so it is possible to point to a single obvious distinction between sedentary and nomadic dialects: all sedentary dialects have voiceless versions of the Classical phoneme noted as /q/: [ʾ] in most cities of Syria and Egypt, [k] for some rural Palestinian dialects, [q] in Iraq and most of North Africa; whereas nomadic dialects have a voiced consonant, typically [g]. This is the only feature that occurs in all nomadic-sedentary contrasts outside of Arabia.

Most sedentary dialects have lost the interdentals, turning them into stops, so that nomadic [t̲], [d̲], and [ḏ̣] (the last a reflex of both ClA /ẓ/ and /ḍ/) are generally [t], [d], and [ḍ] in sedentary dialects. However, there are sedentary groups using the interdentals scattered in the Fertile Crescent, and they survive in the major sedentary dialect of Tunisia.

Sedentary dialects have lost gender distinctions in the plural of verbs and pronouns. Combined with the elimination of dual forms this leads to a great simplification, since, of the thirty-six forms shown on the chart of verbal inflections in 1.411 (Table 3), at least ten are eliminated, and a similar simplification affects the pronouns.

Sedentary dialects have adopted various particles meaning 'belonging to, associated with', which are used in addition to the construct; Mor. /sseyyāra māl lmūdīr/ 'the director's car'; Syr, /ssayyāra tabaεī/ 'my car', where CIA would have /sayyāratu lmudīr/ and /sayyāratī/ only; both /tabaε/ and /māl/ are used with following nouns or pronouns. Another relatively consistent sedentary supplement to the system of particles is a particle used with a verb to express continuous action: Eg. /εammāl/, /εamm/, Mor. /kā/.

3.232 *Eastern and Western Colloquial Arabic*

Whereas the nomadic-sedentary contrast covers the whole of the Arabic-speaking world, preserving the record of two ways of life which have been important throughout the area and of two major stages of Arabic-speaking migration following after the other Semitic migrations of previous centuries, the present-day Arab world is divided into a number of different areas by regional dialect characteristics. These regional variations are very old and were first described in the middle of the tenth century by the geographer al-Muqaddasī. They correspond only roughly to modern political boundaries, so that 'Moroccan Arabic' and 'Syrian Arabic', for example, do not refer to forms of Arabic spoken throughout these countries and contrasting with the forms spoken in neighboring countries, but to the dialect norms of major cities which tend to be regarded as prestige dialects in the areas administered from those cities, even though the surrounding countryside is a patchwork of different dialect forms, some of them nomadic and some of them very close to the dialect of the capital of the neighboring country.

The regional dialects form two main clusters: *Eastern Arabic,* which is spoken throughout the Fertile Crescent; by Syrian and Lebanese emigré communities in the Americas; in all the Arabic-speaking regions of Asia (including enclaves of an Iraqi-like nomadic dialect in the USSR); in Egypt and the Sudan (where Arabic is side by side with various African languages), and in all areas of East Africa which have been partially Arabized by influences down through the Sudan or across the Red Sea and down the coast (the Arabic of Somalia is Yemenite, that of Zanzibar is like Oman); and *Western Arabic*, the dialect spoken in the region referred to as the Maghreb, namely Morocco, Algeria, Tunisia, and most of Libya, filtering down into the French territories of sub-Saharan West Africa. Eastern and Western Arabic meet and mix around Lake Chad. Again, this division can be attached to a single contrasting feature: in the Eastern dialects, the basic ClA pattern of prefixes for the imperfect is retained (see 1.411), simplified only by the elimination of duals and feminine plurals: in the second and third persons, the singular-plural contrast depends on the suffix (third person masc. sing. /y-/ vs. third person masc. pl. /y—u/; second person masc. sing. /t-/ vs. second person masc. pl. /t—u/); while in the first person there is no plural suffix and the contrast is expressed by the prefix (first person sing. /ˀ(a)-/ vs. first person pl. /n-/). In the Western dialects, the /-u/ suffix has been generalized to all persons of the plural, and the 'we' prefix to all first persons, so that the first person singular has the form /n-/ and the plural has /n—u/: Mor. /nsedd/ 'I close' vs. /nseddu/ 'we close'.

There are a number of other, less striking, contrasts:

Western dialects tend to lose /ˀ/, which is much more generally retained in the East; as a result, they have a greater variety of vowel clusters and diphthongs. In all the Western dialects, vocalic changes have been more drastic than in the East: commonly, all short vowels in open syllables have been lost, so that only long syllables (Cv̄ or CvC) survive (e.g. ClA /šarib/ > Mor. /šreb/). The loss of final short vowels resulted everywhere in final clusters: in the East (except Egypt), where these clusters were difficult to pronounce, vowels were inserted: Ir. /ḥarb/ 'war' but /ṣubuḥ/ 'morning', ClA /ṣubḥ/; in the West, wherever this insertion of a vowel after the second consonant took place, it left the first vowel in an open syllable, so that it was dropped: ClA /qabr/ > */qabar/ > Mor. /qbar/ 'tomb'. Furthermore, whereas most Eastern dialects tend to retain /a/ even in positions where /i/ and /u/ are lost, Western does not.

In addition to the special first person forms of the imperfect, Western Arabic has made a number of derivational innovations with, in some cases, new derived verbs rounding out the ClA pattern and a form with prefixed /t-/~/tt-/ functioning like ClA

Form VII: Mor. /tekteb/ (cf. ClA /nkatab/, 'be written'). Because of the slighter revision of the vowel system, Eastern dialects tend, in part, to retain the different vowel patterns of primary verbs: Syr. /btuktub/ 'you write', /btišrab/ 'you drink'.

There are also very striking differences in vocabulary, with items that are used throughout the whole of one dialect area being completely unknown in another.

3.233 *Iraqi Arabic*[12]

The prestige dialect of Iraq, which is the one most likely to be studied by outsiders, is the dialect of the Muslim population of Baghdad. This is one of several dialect varieties spoken in Iraq, some of which extend quite a distance outside of the political boundaries of the country, and which belong to a type of Arabic referred to as Mesopotamian, or 'Eastern Arabic'. This dialect is spoken in a broad band running from Kuwait on the Persian Gulf through all of Iraq and up into Arabic-speaking areas in south-eastern Turkey, including eastern Syria, around Palmyra and as far west as the area of Aleppo; related forms are spoken in southern Iran and in the Soviet Union. Only in Iraq, however, is it the prestige dialect of large metropolitan and administrative centers. In general, the area is characterized by (a) the phonemes /p/, /č/, and /j/ = [dž], which have varying etymologies: all are reinforced by the many Turkish and Iranian loanwords in the dialect, and /k/ appears with varying consistency as the reflex of ClA /k/; (b) the preservation of ClA interdentals and diphthongs (side by side with /ē/ and /ō/) over most of the area; (c) various reflexes of ClA /q/ (but never /ˀ/); (d) the preservation of /-n/ after the long vowel suffixes of the imperfect: /yisuknūn/ 'they live', /trīdīn/ 'you (fem.) wish' vs. ClA /yaskunūn/ and /turīdīn/; (e) a characteristic construction suffixing the appropriate pronoun to a transitive verb and then prefixing /l-/ to the noun object: /ma aḥibba lhāḏa/ 'I don't like this one', where /aḥibb/ is 'I like' and /-a/ is the dialectal form of the third person singular pronoun suffix (ClA /-hu/); (f) characteristic lexical items, such as /fadd/ 'a, an (indefinite article)', and /māl/ 'belonging to' (as an alternative to the construct); and throughout the lexicon. Iraq is often called 'the land of /aku/ and /māku/', which mean 'there is' and 'there is not' in this region. Other words special to this dialect area are /hassa/ 'now', /mēz/ 'table', and /bazzūna/ 'cat', as well as a very large number of Turkish and Persian loans[13].

The Muslim dialect of Baghdad, while it clearly belongs to the Iraqi regional type, is a nomadic dialect, with a voiced reflex of ClA /q/: /gelet/ 'I said' (cf. ClA /qultu/). Sedentary dialects, still spoken in the historic cities of the north of Iraq, Mosul, Tikrīt, etc., and in the sedentary regions of eastern Syria, have /qeltu/ 'I said'. These dialects dominated the area until the drastic breakdown of urban control, with accompanying anarchy and nomadic invasions, after the sack of Baghdad in 1258; this trend continued for five centuries, and when the tide turned in the eighteenth century and city life began to develop again, the old sedentary Muslim populations were so heavily infiltrated by speakers of nomadic dialects that their dialects were Bedouinized. In Upper Iraq, the devastation was slighter and /qeltu/ dialects are still used by settled populations; in Lower Iraq, /qeltu/ dialects only survived among Jewish and Christian minority groups (see 3.237). In general, the phonology of the Baghdad dialect is more like ClA, whereas the old sedentary dialects have /č/ for ClA /k/ in many environments, /ġ/ for ClA /r/, and more *imāla* (inclination of /a/ toward /i/): Baghdad /jāmeε/ 'mosque' vs. Mosul /jēme ε/.

3.234 *Syrian Arabic*

Syrian Arabic is a construct based on the remarkably similar dialects spoken by the population of several important cities of eastern Syria, Palestine, and Lebanon, especially Damascus, Jerusalem, and Beirut; it is sometimes referred to as Eastern Mediterranean Arabic and is the prestige dialect of Syria, Lebanon, and Jordan. Urban settlement has been more stable in this area, and although nomadic dialects are used in a few places in the country and in the desert areas, agricultural towns and villages speak dialects going back to the koine. These city dialects have /ˀ/ for ClA /q/, /k/ for ClA /k/, /j/=[ž], and have completely lost the interdentals, which have become /t/, /d/, and /ḍ/. Long /ā/ has been stable and short /a/ has been relatively stable everywhere except in the feminine ending, which has *imāla:*

/madrase/ 'school', ClA /madrasah/. The loss of diphthongs, which have only survived as doubled semivowels, and otherwise have been simplified to /ē/ and /ō/, e.g. /bēt/ 'house', ClA /bayt/, occurred in this area except in a large part of Lebanon. Corresponding to the specific lexical items cited for Iraq, Syrian Arabic has: /fī/, /mā fī/, 'there is', 'there is not'; /wāḥid/ 'a, an' for the indefinite article; /tabaɛ/ (~/šīt/ in Damascus, /šēt/ in Jerusalem) 'belonging to'; /halla/ or /hallaˀ/ 'now'; /ṭāwla/ 'table'; and /bisse/ 'cat'; the last two forms are derived from ClA. Syrian Arabic contrasts with ClA and with most other dialects, which would use an auxiliary verb, in using /bidd-/ with suffixed pronoun to express a wish: /biddī ˀarūḥ/ 'I want to go'.

3.235 *Egyptian Arabic*

Egyptian Arabic is more similar to Syrian Arabic than the latter is to Iraqi, for it is also an Oriental sedentary dialect—that is, both fall on the same side of the East-West contrast and the sedentary-nomadic contrast. In Upper (southern) Egypt, Bedouinized dialects are spoken which contrast quite radically with the prestige dialect of Cairo, but the Cairene influence is spreading.

Cairene Arabic contrasts with Syrian Arabic in that it has ClA /j/=[g]: Egypt is the 'land of the gīm', and although ClA /q/ has become /ˀ/ in all true colloquial words, there are more Classical loans in common usage, so that /q/ is quite frequent. Egyptian Arabic also has a stress pattern which contrasts with Syrian: Eg. /madrása/ 'school' vs. Syr. /mádrase/. In general, Syrian accent falls on the v̄C or vCC nearest the end of the word or, if no such sequence appears, on the first syllable. In Egyptian, the same syllable types would draw the accent to the final syllable; otherwise it generally falls on the penultimate syllable.

For the lexical items already mentioned: /wāḥid/ 'a, an', /fī/, /ma fīš/ 'there is', 'there is not' (š appears for negation in many varieties of Oriental Arabic); /bitāɛ/~/mitāɛ/ 'belonging to'; /dilwaˀti/ 'now' (Egyptian Arabic is the only major city dialect that has lost the /hā-/ of the ClA demonstratives; cf. ClA /hād̲ā lwaqt/ 'this time'); /ṭarabēẓa/ 'table'; /ˀuṭṭa/ 'cat'. Egyptians tend to be highly amused by the /xāṭrak/ with which Syrians begin the series of polite formulae that accompany departure, since this is never used in Egypt.

3.236 *North African Arabic*

Dialect boundaries in the Maghreb do not correspond particularly well with political boundaries and are better explained with reference to the linguistic layers that have affected the whole North African littoral. Unlike the countries that have been discussed so far, the language which was in use before the Arab invasions is still in extensive use: there are four million speakers of Berber in Morocco, two and a half million in Algeria, and much smaller numbers in Tunisia and Libya; Berber speakers are concentrated in the back country, and their influence shows primarily in rural dialects of Arabic such as in the mountainous areas of Morocco: odd variants of the dentals, [ts] or [t^y], and a great deal of loan vocabulary. North Africa was conquered by the Arabs in the seventh and eighth centuries, but only some 150,000 troops settled there, while the greater number pressed on to Spain. North Africa was thinly settled and the Arabs stayed in cities like Tangier along the coast, although some of these settlements were later pushed to rural areas such as Jbala. Later, when Spain was reconquered by the Christians, Muslims left in wave after wave of exiles, establishing new dynasties and founding some new cities, like Fez, further in the interior. Old Arabic dialects in North Africa, then, show various degrees of Berber influence and reflect two strands of dialect descended from the koine, one of which developed in Spain, while the other developed in various pockets of settlement among those who did not move on to Spain. Nomadic Arabic swept across North Africa in the eleventh and twelfth centuries, brought by Beni Hilal tribesmen from southern Arabia, estimated at about 200,000, and other tribal groups have followed. Some cities, e.g. Gabès in Tunisia, Marrakesh in Morocco, or Oran and towns near Algiers in Algeria, speak Bedouin dialects, often with non-Muslim minorities still preserving the old urban dialects descended from the koine, but the majority of urban centers retain urban dialects, many rural areas show strong Bedouin influences, and the whole nomadic Arabic-speaking population speaks nomadic type Arabic. The nomadic and urban speakers must strain to understand each other.

There is of course considerable variation from city to city. The urban dialects of Libya and some parts of Tunisia reduce ClA /j/ to [z] in some contexts: /zūz/ 'pair', ClA /zawj/. Tunisian dialects seem to have considerable short vowel variation, and have omitted the very common development of an indefinite article (developed from variations on /wāḥid/ elsewhere) and a substitute for *iḍāfa*. Moroccan forms for the other lexical items that have been mentioned are /kāy^{e}n/, /ma kāy^{e}nš/ 'there is', 'there is not'; /d-/~/dyāl/~/mtāε/ 'of, belonging to'; /mīda/ 'table'; and /qeṭṭa/ 'cat'.

The dialect spoken on the island of Malta, which is now completely Christian and was for some time a British Protectorate after a long period of Italian rule, seems to be a variant of North African urban Arabic. Maltese has suffered such a flood of Italian loanwords and is so drastically distorted in its phonology and syntax that it was once considered no more than a very strange and deviant dialect of Italian. However, the morphology is quite clearly descended from koine Arabic. Maltese is of some interest because it is a form of Colloquial Arabic which has been completely separated from any ClA influence; it is written in a special Latin letter alphabet designed for it, and is beginning to produce some literature. Even in the Soviet Union, where Arabic speakers now have a Cyrillic orthography for their dialects and are encouraged to use it, some Classical influence is maintained.

3.237 *Communal dialects*

In the history of some cities of the Arab world, dialectal shifts have taken place which have left religious minorities speaking special dialects. These are at present usually Christian minorities since in most places the Jewish colonies that were equally affected by this split are either in Israel, where their special Arabic dialects may be expected to die out, or they are doing their best to be inconspicuous, which may mean adopting the majority dialect. In most places the separate community life of the minority has fostered slight dialect differences, especially in vocabulary (the Jews have tended to use a good deal of Hebrew vocabulary), and the greater tendency of Christians to be educated in European-sponsored schools may foster special loanwords, so that is is often possible to recognize members of minority communities by their speech, although many Christians or Jews have learned to control the majority dialect and may boast that they can 'speak like a Muslim' in the market. In most places the minority populations are urban and really drastic differences only develop as a result of major shifts in population such as the Bedouinization of Lower Iraq and some North African cities.

3.24 *Influences of Classical Arabic and interdialectal influences*

There are a number of points at which Classical forms regularly invade CoA. Throughout the Arab world, there are formulae which may be pronounced in partial conformity with the phonology of the region but preserve ClA case endings. Many of these are formal phrases of etiquette, since Arabic is particularly rich in sequences of polite remarks each having an appropriate response, sometimes forming a whole chain: appropriate wishes for each time of day; phrases to be used in greeting someone who is eating, someone who has just had a drink, someone who has bathed or had a haircut; phrases used to ward off misfortune when admiring something or inquiring about someone's family; extravagant offers of hospitality. Others are curses or exclamations. CoA also borrows a great deal of vocabulary from ClA. Educated speakers draw on the education they have received in a Classical context whenever they are discussing technical or academic subjects, and many such words enter the general vocabulary, sometimes via the radio or cinema. Much religious vocabulary is borrowed from ClA: in Jerusalem, for instance, where ClA /q/ normally becomes /ˀ/, /q/ is still pronounced in the word /qurˀān/, and Cairo Arabic has a considerable number of ClA loanwords preserving /q/. The same Classical word may have two cognates in CoA, one of which has followed the normal evolution of the dialect while the other has been borrowed. In areas where the interdentals are reduced to dentals by the dialect they are pronounced as sibilants in Classical loanwords, so that ClA /ḥadiṯ/ 'event, saying' yields both /ḥadīt/ 'event' and

/ḥadīs/ 'saying attributed to Muḥammad'. Proverbs, including religious maxims, are often quoted in ClA, and a number of recognizable ClA proverbs are part of the inventory of illiterate speakers.

Influences between the dialects tend to occur in relation to the prestige dialect of an area, so that there is a tendency for the dialect of the capital to spread into the surrounding countryside, since it is generally necessary to learn it in order to participate in the national life, and for non-Muslims to imitate the Muslim dialect. This tends toward the enhancement of the dialect of the capital and an increasing tendency for dialect boundaries to correspond to national boundaries. Egyptian Arabic, through radio broadcasting and films, is the only sedentary dialect which is presently influencing other regions. There is also a continuing tendency among young people in poor rural areas to imitate nearby Bedouin groups.

Because of the difficulties of diglossia, there has been a good deal of talk about the possibilities of developing a 'middle language', a form of Arabic which would lack the complexities of ClA and yet be understandable throughout the Arab world and maintain contact with the Classical tradition. At present, intellectuals from different Arab countries have several alternatives in speaking to each other: (a) they may speak or try to speak ClA, which imposes a great deal of strain and formalism; (b) they may speak French or English; or (c) they may try to use their own forms of CoA for a maximum of communication. Their education gives them the resources for this last which might be impossible to villagers from the same regions. The principal means of educated interdialectal conversation have been described as 'classicizing' and 'leveling'[14]. 'Classicizing' may be very superficial, using items which are associated with educated speech even within a dialect region but do not add much to the communicative value: introducing clauses with /ˀan/ without changing their basic syntax, restoring some short vowels and /q/, and using /fa-/ frequently although all the dialects have /wa-/. Classical vocabulary is freely borrowed, as it is in all educated (and pretentious) speech. 'Leveling' involves underplaying those features of the speaker's dialect which are known to be aberrant or are considered so in the Arabs' mythology about their dialects and selecting among alternatives those features which are most like ClA. Often leveling takes place more in relation to the prestige dialect of the speaker's own region than to the dialect of his companion. Leveling may take place without particular reference to ClA, as in the kind of 'normalized Bedouin' which was spoken by nomadic recruits from different tribal areas while they did army service during the French occupation of Syria,[15] and suggests one process which must have been operative in the formation of the koine.

3.25 *The use of Colloquial Arabic*

Colloquial Arabic is used in all of the contexts which do not demand the use of Classical. At first glance, these may seem quite limited, but in fact they make up the major part of life: CoA is the only language of a great many inhabitants of Arab countries; it is used in almost all conversation with servants or workmen, in the street or in the market, and in most informal conversation with colleagues even in academic or political circles. Most important, CoA is the only language which is ever used in the home, and Arabs who advocate the complete adoption of ClA find the idea of speaking it to their own children ludicrous. On the other hand, because CoA is felt to lack eloquence and structure, children receive little or no formal training in manipulating it. Between a quarter and a half of the total time in elementary school is spent on gaining a bare mastery of Classical Arabic. Modern methods have brought some concern for developing the child's ability to order and express his thought, side by side with the traditional training in rhetoric which accompanies reading and writing, grammar and memorization, but almost none of this time is spent on developing language skills in the actual spoken language. CoA is the mother tongue of the Arab and remains throughout his life the primary medium of interpersonal relationships, especially intimate ones, but it is never developed as the medium for abstract thought. Many Arabs use both CoA and ClA, but their knowledge of each is specialized and their fluency is always situational; the use of the wrong variety in a particular situation is felt as extremely inappropriate. However, many Arabs do feel that their local dialect is closer to the Classical than any other.

CoA invades the specifically Classical spheres of broadcasting, literature, and publishing in a number of circumscribed ways: it may be used for dialogue in radio plays or movies and often in print, especially in the captions of cartoons or in humorous or anecdotal material. Writing Colloquial in the Arabic alphabet is governed by fluctuating conventions, but the normalization implied by the omission of the vowels and so on, makes written CoA appear to deviate less from ClA than it actually does. In conservative transcriptions the article is usually written according to the ClA convention (always with the letter for /l/ since the assimilation to following apicals is automatic), and the feminine ending is indicated by the letter for /h/. Because of the differences in phonology, Western scholars now almost always use a transcription based on latin letter forms for writing CoA, which may or may not reflect a full phonological analysis of the dialect.

There are also several branches of Arabic literature where CoA is the norm, although historically these have been outside of the main stream. First of all, the composition and recitation of poetry has remained a part of nomadic life, usually in slightly different dialectal form from that used in actual speech and closely surrounded by convention. Rural sedentary areas have also developed rich folklore traditions, with a slightly wider range, including songs and some semi-dramatic forms. Most of what we possess of this folk literature has been collected by Western orientalists or linguists, but there has been some interest in this tradition on the part of Arabs, especially where, as in Lebanon, the Pan-Arab identification is low and there is an interest in regional folk traditions and collections of songs and proverbs have been made. Some of this interest has gone even further and combined with the unease many Arab writers feel about writing dialogue or describing domestic or village life in ClA, so that a number of writers have experimented with novels or plays in CoA, vacillating between ClA and CoA, or even issuing their work in two versions, one in CoA and one in ClA, for wider circulation in other dialect areas. There were two movements toward a written literary production in CoA in the medieval period: a vulgar poetry of the cities of Iraq and songs, especially of the type called *zajal*, in Andalusia and North Africa.

Not surprisingly, the influence of the ClA norm has been weaker among non-Muslim minorities. CoA appears in texts written by Christians and Jews living under Arab Islamic rule as early as the ninth century; these were primarily non-literary prose texts which reflect efforts to approximate ClA by populations which had not fully mastered it and were clearly speaking forms of Arabic very like the present-day urban dialects. Since they are all in the Arabic alphabet and attempt to follow ClA norms, the features of this 'Middle Arabic'[16] have to be deduced from errors and from hypercorrect forms, but it seems clear that Middle Arabic had already lost the final short vowels, with the stabilization of word order this implies, reduced its inflectional categories (duals only in the noun, a single relative pronoun), etc. Most of the recognizable features of Middle Arabic are those which are attributed to the koine and characterize modern and sedentary dialects in general, although there is some local variation and a slight variation between Christian and Jewish texts. Many leaders in the modernization of ClA were Christians who stressed their right to a full Arab identity through the language, but in some areas, especially Lebanon, North Africa, and the Yemen, the ClA norm has been weaker for Christians and Jews, who have been more apt to write CoA forms.

3.3 Speech and writing in other languages

In the Arab world, a number of other languages are used. These fall into two categories: indigenous minority languages which, for their speakers, precede the knowledge of Arabic necessary for full participation in the national life; and European languages which are learned as second (or third) languages by both speakers of Arabic and speakers of the minority languages, and open up the possibilities of education and communication in terms of European culture. The most important indigenous languages are:

(1) *Berber* (see 3.236), a distant relative of Arabic which was the old language of North Africa and is still spoken by a third of

the population of Morocco and a fifth of that of Algeria. Berber is not used administratively and is actively discouraged by the Arab governments. In most areas it is purely a spoken language, but the roman alphabet has been adopted in Kabylia and there is a certain amount of popular literature.

(2) *Kurdish*, the Indo-European language of the Kurds which is closely related to Persian. The Kurds live in a number of different countries, including Iran, Turkey, and the Soviet Union, but the largest group in any Arabic-speaking country is in northern Iraq. Kurdish tribesmen have been in rebellion against the central government for a number of years, and one of the issues has been the possibility of using their language in administration and in higher education. There is some publishing in Kurdish, using the Arabic alphabet, in Iraq. A modified Cyrillic alphabet is used by Kurdish speakers in the Soviet Union and large quantities of written and broadcast revolutionary propaganda in Kurdish originate there, but the body of literature in Kurdish is quite small.

(3) *Armenian*, another Indo-European language with no close relatives within that superfamily. Small groups of Armenian merchants established colonies in most of the large cities of the Middle East during the period of the Ottoman Empire, and there is a very old colony in Jerusalem, but the large colonies that can now be found in Syria, especially in Aleppo, and around Beirut are mainly composed of survivors of the Turkish deportations during World War I when hundreds of thousands of Armenians were driven into the Syrian desert. Armenian has two principal dialects, one (Eastern Armenian) spoken by Armenians living in and around the present Soviet Socialist Republic of Armenia and in Iran, and the other (Western Armenian) spoken by Armenians descended from the subjects of the medieval Armenian kingdom of Cilicia which was founded by a group of Armenians that migrated to Asia Minor, outside of traditional Armenian territory. The Turkish oppressions destroyed the population concentrations in present-day Turkish territory, but there is a contemporary cultural center of western Armenians in the Arab world. Armenians run schools (which are now required to

dedicate a great deal of time to Arabic), publish newspapers, and carry on a considerable literary production; large quarters of some cities, especially Beirut and Jerusalem, are Armenian. Classical Armenian is the liturgical language of the Armenian Apostolic Church, and there are also Protestant and Eastern-rite Catholic groups using the language and maintaining important establishments. Unlike the Berbers and the Kurds, the Armenians are richer and better educated than the Muslims around them; their participation in government is limited in some places, but they produce many merchants and professional men, including many of the doctors.

(4) A number of other languages of less importance are still used: *South Arabic* (see 2.1) survives in a small region along the southern coast of Arabia. *Syriac-Aramaic* (see 2.1) includes *Classical Syriac*, which is used liturgically by a number of Eastern churches; *Neo-Syriac*, a language spoken by a number of non-Muslims in Iran and Iraq; and *Aramaic*, in a few pockets in the Syrian dialect area. *Coptic* is used liturgically in Egypt but has not been spoken for several centuries, and there are a few speakers of *Turkmen* or of the *Turkish* of Turkey, and of *Circassian*, a Caucasian language.

For all of these indigenous languages, although there may be large numbers of speakers who know no Arabic, the majority of these are women, while the men have learned at least a minimal amount of Arabic for dealing with the government. The Armenians will probably carry on an autonomous cultural life for a long time to come, but there is no proposal to set up separate administrative districts for them. There might be a great practical gain in extending the use of Berber and Kurdish, but the Arab governments are uniformly opposed to this.

There is also widespread knowledge of European languages in the Arab world, depending on the occupying countries during the period after World War I: in most of North Africa and in Syria and Lebanon, French is the prevailing European language; both French and English have been important in Egypt; and in the Sudan, Arabia, Jordan, and Iraq, English has a greater influence.

Italian is the commonest second language of Libya but the influence of English is increasing, and Spanish is known in Spanish Morocco. The knowledge of a major European language is everywhere an advantage, but in North Africa this has been carried to a point where it threatens the Arab identity of the country[17]. During the French occupation, the number of European settlers exceeded the number of Arabs who originally Arabized North Africa, and the French made every effort to discourage Arabic culture. One-third of the population of Morocco and a half of the populations of Algeria and Tunisia speak French, and more people are literate in French than in Arabic. French is extensively used in the schools and in government and although the present policy is in favor of Arabization, the North African leaders want to retain French and the access to French culture and lack sufficient trained Arabs to maintain an effective Arabization program.

In the French-influenced countries of the Levant this has not occurred because there was never an extensive colonization and the term of French control was shorter. Whereas in North Africa no higher education or participation in government is possible for a monolingual, it is now fully possible to study such fields as law or medicine in Arabic at Arab universities in Cairo, Alexandria, Baghdad, and Damascus; literacy in Arabic is higher, and, except for minority groups like the Armenians and some Christian Arabs, literacy in Arabic normally precedes literacy in French. Many Christians maintain their knowledge of French as part of their identification with Europe, and an ability to speak French is a mark of the educated bourgeoisie, but it is not the only way of gaining access to a general education. English has penetrated even less, so that nowhere in the region where Eastern dialects are spoken is there any question but that Arabic is the primary medium of literacy for the Muslim population.

NOTES

1. Chaim Rabin, *Ancient West Arabian* (London, 1951).
2. The outstanding example of this is the *melhūn*, a classicized and Bedouinized dialect used in North Africa for poetry; cf.

G. Colin, 'L'arabe', in *Initiation au Maroc*, ed. Louis Brunot (Paris, 1945), p. 225. For similar examples, cf. R. Blachère, *Histoire de la littérature arabe* (Paris, 1952), p. 80.

3. Johann Fück, *'Arabīya, Recherches sur l'histoire de la langue et du style arabe*, tr. Claude Denizeau (Paris, 1955).
4. Charles A. Ferguson, 'Diglossia', *Word* 15.325–40 (1959).
5. UNESCO, *World Illiteracy at Mid-Century* (Paris, 1957).
6. Most of the examples in this section are taken from Vincent Monteil, *L'arabe moderne* (Paris, 1960).
7. Richard S. Harrell, *Contributions to Arabic Linguistics*, ed. Charles A. Ferguson (Cambridge, Mass., 1960) p. 9, 15.
8. Similar problems and processes have been described for modern Hebrew by Haim Blanc in 'Hebrew in Israel: Trends and Problems', *Middle East Journal* 11.397–409 (1957).
9. Anwar Chejne, 'The Role of Arabic in Present-Day Arab Society', *The Islamic Literature* 10:4.15–54 (1958).
10. Charles A. Ferguson, 'The Arabic Koine', *Language* 35.616–30 (1959); and David Cohen, 'Koinè, langues communes et dialectes arabes', *Arabica* 9.119–44 (1962).
11. Jean Cantineau, *Cours de phonétique arabe* (Paris, 1960).
12. Haim Blanc, *Communal Dialects in Baghdad* (Cambridge, Mass., 1964).
13. Charles A. Ferguson and Majed Sa'īd, 'Lexical Variants in Arabic Dialects' [1958, mimeo.] has been used for almost all the lexical examples.
14. Haim Blanc, 'Stylistic Variations in Spoken Arabic: A Sample of Interdialectal Conversation', in Charles A. Ferguson (ed.) *Contributions to Arabic Linguistics* (Cambridge, Mass., 1960), pp. 81–156.
15. Jean Cantineau, *Le dialecte arabe de Palmyre* (Beirut, 1934).
16. Yehoshua Blau, 'The Importance of Middle Arabic Dialects for the History of Arabic', *Studies in Islamic History and Civilization, Scripta Hierosolymitana* 9.206–28 (Jerusalem, 1961).
17. Charles F. Gallagher, 'The Language Problem in North Africa', *North Africa: State and Society 1964* (18th Annual Conference of the Middle East Institute, unpublished papers).

BIBLIOGRAPHY

The following sources for the study of Arabic have been selected from the great mass of existing materials to provide readily available further reading, including beginning textbooks, on topics which are most likely to be of interest to American students of Arabic or to linguists. For convenience, very few periodical references are included and almost all works in foreign languages have been omitted.

A. CLASSICAL ARABIC

W. Wright, *A Grammar of the Arabic Language,* 3rd ed., 2 vols., Cambridge, Cambridge University Press, 1955. This is the basic reference grammar for Classical Arabic and has been a standard text for more than a century. It is rather cumbersome, leaning heavily on the Arab grammatical tradition.

Hans Wehr, *A Dictionary of Modern Written Arabic,* ed. J Milton Cowan, Ithaca, N.Y., Cornell University Press, 1961. A basic dictionary of the vocabulary in current use in the Arab world. Two other dictionaries are often recommended for beginning students:

Elias A. Elias, *School Dictionary: Arabic-English, English-Arabic,* Cairo, Elias Modern Press [no date]. Laconic and dated, but contains an English-Arabic section; and:

J.G. Hava, *Arabic-English Dictionary,* rev. ed., Beirut, Catholic Press, 1963. The best small dictionary for early Arabic and poetry.

There are a number of textbooks available, differing both in method and in the type of material they prepare the student to read, and more appear every year:

G.W. Thatcher, *Arabic Grammar of the Written Language,* New York, Frederick Ungar, [reprint ed., no date]. Several generations of Arabists started with this text and it remains the best text for a reading knowledge of pre-Modern Arabic. It has now been largely superseded by the following:

J.A. Haywood and H.M. Nahmad, *A New Arabic Grammar of the Written Language,* Cambridge, Mass., Harvard University Press, 1962. An inferior revised version of Thatcher which includes a great deal of contemporary vocabulary. Both Thatcher and Haywood and Nahmad are available with keys to the exercises.

More fashionable approaches emphasize the development of an active control of the language and usually presuppose the assistance of a native speaker and time spent listening to tapes. Texts of this genre include:

Farhat J. Ziadeh and R. Bayly Winder, *An Introduction to Modern Arabic,* Princeton, N.J., Princeton University Press, 1957 [records and tapes available].

Ernest N. McCarus and Adil I. Yacoub, *Elements of Contemporary Arabic: Part I,* Ann Arbor, Mich., Ann Arbor Publishers, 1962 [tapes available].

Daud Atiyeh Abdo, *A Course in Modern Standard Arabic,* 2 vols., Beirut, Khayats, 1962–64 [tapes available].

Charles A. Ferguson and Moukhtar Ani, *Lessons in Contemporary Arabic: Lessons 1–8,* rev. ed., Washington, D.C., Center for Applied Linguistics, 1964 [tapes available].

All of the texts include discussion of the Arabic script, but a more detailed treatment may be found in the following:

T.F. Mitchell, *Writing Arabic: A Practical Introduction to the Ruq'ah Script,* London, Oxford University Press, 1953.

Frank A. Rice, *The Classical Arabic Writing System,* Cambridge, Mass., Harvard University Press, 1959.

B. COLLOQUIAL ARABIC

Harvey Sobelman, ed., *Arabic Dialect Studies: A Selected Bibliography,* Washington, D.C., Center for Applied Linguistics and the Middle East Institute, 1962. An evaluated list of significant scholarly work as well as textbooks published on the following dialects: Syrian, Egyptian, Arabian Peninsula, Iraqi, North African, and Maltese. Since publication of this bibliography a series of reference grammars and dictionaries have appeared in the Arabic Series of the School of Languages and Linguistics, Georgetown University, Washington, D.C.:

Richard S. Harrell, *A Short Reference Grammar of Moroccan Arabic,* 1962.

Wallace M. Erwin, *A Short Reference Grammar of Iraqi Arabic,* 1963.

Mark W. Cowell, *A Short Reference Grammar of Syrian Arabic,* 1964.

Harvey Sobelman and Richard S. Harrell, *A Dictionary of Moroccan Arabic: English-Moroccan,* 1963.

Beverly E. Clarity *et al., A Dictionary of Iraqi Arabic: English-Iraqi,* 1964.

Karl Stowasser and Moukhtar Ani, *A Dictionary of Syrian Arabic: English-Syrian,* 1964.

The Moroccan-English, Iraqi-English, and Syrian-English volumes are forthcoming. The Series also includes introductory courses for two of these dialects (see below). Further sources for the dialects follow.

(1) *Syrian area*

Charles A. Ferguson with the assistance of Moukhtar Ani and others, *Damascus Arabic,* Washington, D.C., Center for Applied Linguistics, 1961 [reprint of materials developed in the fifties for the Foreign Service Institute].

Frank A. Rice and Majed F. Sa'id, *Eastern Arabic: An Introduction to the Spoken Arabic of Palestine, Syria and Lebanon,* Beirut, Khayats, 1960 [tapes available].

(2) *Egyptian area*

T.F. Mitchell, *An Introduction to Colloquial Egyptian Arabic,* London, Oxford University Press, 1956.

Richard S. Harrell *et al.*, *Lessons in Colloquial Egyptian Arabic,* rev. ed., 1963 (Georgetown Arabic Series [see above]) [tapes available].

Walter Lehn and Peter Abboud, *Beginning Cairo Arabic,* Austin, Texas, 1965 [order from Hemphill's Book Stores, Austin, Texas; tapes available].

Dictionaries present something of a problem for Egyptian Arabic. The following are the most promising:

Socrates Spiro Bey, *Arabic-English Dictionary of the Modern Arabic of Egypt,* 2nd ed., Cairo, 1923.

———, *An English-Arabic Vocabulary of the Modern and Colloquial Arabic of Egypt,* 3rd ed., Cairo, 1929.

Edward E. Elias, *Practical Dictionary of the Colloquial Arabic of the Middle East: English-Arabic,* 2nd ed., Cairo, 1949.

(3) *Saudi Arabia*

The Arabian American Oil Company has published in its Aramco Arabic Language Series a number of texts and phrasebooks primarily based on the dialect of al-Hasa on the east coast. The vocabulary lists are the best available substitute for a dictionary. The principal books in the Aramco series are:

Pocket Guide to Arabic, 1955.

Conversational Arabic [no date].

Basic Arabic, 1957.

Spoken Arabic, 1957 [accompanying records].

English-Arabic Work List, 1958.

Work Arabic, 1954- [a series of manuals dealing with technical vocabulary, e.g. medicine, transportation, etc.]

(4) *Iraq*

Merrill Y. Van Wagoner, *Spoken Iraqi Arabic,* 2 vols., New York, Holt, Rinehart & Winston, 1949 [records available].

Wallace M. Erwin, *A Basic Course in Iraqi Arabic,* forthcoming (Georgetown Arabic Series [see above]).

(5) *North Africa*

The great mass of publications on North African Arabic are in French and the few translations of text materials that have been made for particular programs are generally available, if at all, only in mimeographed form. For a survey of the literature see *Arabic Dialect Studies,* cited above. Only one modern text is widely available:

Richard S. Harrell *et al., A Basic Course in Moroccan Arabic,* 1965 (Georgetown Arabic Series [see above]) [tapes available].

(6) Maltese

There are two good introductory texts for Maltese: Aquilina is the more appropriate for the student with no knowledge of any form of Arabic, while Sutcliffe builds on a prior knowledge, drawing many comparisons:

E.F. Sutcliffe, *A Grammar of the Maltese Language with Chrestomathy and Vocabulary,* London, 1936.

Joseph Aquilina, *Teach Yourself Maltese,* London, English Universities Press, 1965.

V. Busuttil, *Dizzjunarju mill-Malti ghall-Inglis* [Maltese-English Dictionary], rev. ed., Malta, 1942.

English-Maltese Dictionary, Government of Malta, 1946.

C. ARABIC LITERATURE

There are a number of discursive histories of Arabic or other Islamic literatures which include extensive quotes from authors discussed here, along with background material and bibliographies:

H.A.R. Gibb, *Arabic Literature,* 2nd ed., Oxford, The Clarendon Press, 1963.

R.A. Nicholson, *A Literary History of the Arabs,* Cambridge, Cambridge University Press, 1956.

Edward C. Browne, *A Literary History of Persia,* 4 vols., Cambridge, Cambridge University Press, 1956. For Arabic, see especially vols. 1 and 2.

Arthur J. Arberry, *Sufism: An Account of the Mystics of Islam,* London, George Allen & Unwin, 1950.

Two sources of literary criticism and analysis should be mentioned here as they go beyond the philological and historical study which have been traditional:

H.A.R. Gibb, *Studies on the Civilization of Islam,* ed. S.J. Shaw and W.R. Polk, Boston, Beacon Press, 1962. See especially no. 7, 'Tarikh', an analysis of Islamic historiography; no. 12, 'Reflections on Arabic Literature', a study of the development of Arabic prose style; and no. 13, 'Studies in Contemporary Arabic Literature'.

Gustav E. von Grunebaum, 'The Aesthetic Foundation of Arabic Literature', *Comparative Literature* 1952, pp. 323–40.

Lastly, there are many translations of whole works or of sections of prose works brought together in anthologies. Only a very few of these can be mentioned here.

Mohammed Marmaduke Pickthall, *The Meaning of the Glorious Koran: An Explanatory Translation,* Mentor Religious Classics, New York, 1958.

James Kritzeck, ed., *Anthology of Islamic Literature,* New York, Holt, Rinehart & Winston, 1964.

R.A. Nicholson, *Translations of Eastern Poetry and Prose,* Cambridge, Cambridge University Press, 1921.

A.J. Arberry, *Modern Arabic Poetry,* London, 1950.

Supplementary Bibliography on Arabic Language

This updated bibliography contains reference works in English and French on both Classical and Modern Standard Arabic, some widely used Arabic textbooks, and a few introductory texts on Arabic literature.

Reference Works

Bakalla, M. H. 1975. *Arabic Linguistics: An Introduction and Bibliography*. London: Mansell.

Beeston, A. F. L. 1970. *The Arabic Language Today*. London: Hutchinson University Library.

Blachère, R. and M. Gaudefroy-Demombynes. 1975. *Grammaire de l'arabe classique: Morphologie et syntax*. Paris: Maisonneuve & Larose.

Cantarino, Vicente. 1974–76. *The Syntax of Modern Arabic Prose*. 3 vols. Bloomington: Indiana University Press.

Doniach, N. S., ed. 1972. *The Oxford English-Arabic Dictionary of Current Usage*. Oxford: Clarendon Press.

Fischer, Wolfdietrich. 2002. *A Grammar of Classical Arabic*. Third revised edition. Trans. by Jonathan Rogers. New Haven and London: Yale University Press.

Holes, Clive. 1995. *Modern Arabic: Structures, Functions and Varieties*. London: Longman.

Howell, Mortimer Sloper. 1986 (reprint). *A Grammar of the Classical Arabic Language*. 4 vols. in 7. New Delhi: Gian Publishing.

Kouloughli, D. E. 1994. *Grammaire de l'arabe d'aujourd'hui*. Paris: Pocket.

LeComte, Gerard. 1968. *Grammaire de l'arabe*. Paris: Presses Universitaires de France. (This book is particularly useful for concise explanations of morphological structure.)

Moscati, Sabatino. 1969. *An Introduction to Comparative Grammar of the Semitic Languages*. Weisbaden: Harrassowitz.

Ryding, Karin C. (forthcoming). *A Basic Reference Grammar of Modern Standard Arabic*. Cambridge: Cambridge University Press.

Versteegh, Kees. 1997. *The Arabic Language*. New York: Columbia University Press.

Textbooks

Abboud, Peter F., Ernest N. McCarus, et al. 1968. *Elementary Modern Standard Arabic,* Parts One and Two. Cambridge: Cambridge University Press.

Abboud, Peter F., Aman Attieh, Ernest McCarus, and Raji M. Rammuny. 1997. *Intermediate Modern Standard Arabic,* (rev. edit.). Ann Arbor, MI.: Center for Middle Eastern and North African Studies.

Alosh, Mahdi. 2000. *Ahlan wa-sahlan: Functional Modern Standard Arabic for Beginners*. New Haven, Conn.: Yale University Press.

Baccouche, Belkacem, and Sanaa Azmi. 1984. *Conversations in Modern Standard Arabic*. New Haven, Conn.: Yale University Press.

Brustad, Kristen, Mahmoud Al-Batal, and Abbas al-Tonsi. 1995. *Alif-Baa: Introduction to Arabic Letters and Sounds.* Washington. D.C.: Georgetown University Press.

———. 1995. *Al-Kitâb fii ta^{c}allum al-^{c}arabiyya: A Textbook for Arabic,* Part One. Washington, D.C.: Georgetown University Press.

———.1997. *Al-Kitâb fii ta^{c}allum al-^{c}arabiyya: A Textbook for Arabic,* Part Two. Washington, D.C.: Georgetown University Press.

———. 2001. *Al-Kitâb fii ta^{c}allum al-^{c}arabiyya: A Textbook for Arabic,* Part Three. Washington, D.C.: Georgetown University Press.

Dickens, James, and Janet C. E. Watson.1998. *Standard Arabic: An Advanced Course*. Cambridge: Cambridge University Press.

McCarus, Ernest, and Raji Rammuny. 1974. *A Programmed Course in Modern Literary Arabic Phonology and Script*. Ann Arbor, Mich.: University of Michigan, Department of Near Eastern Studies.

Middle East Centre for Arab Studies (MECAS), Shemlan, Lebanon. 1965. *The M.E.C.A.S. Grammar of Modern Literary Arabic*. Beirut: Khayats.

Ryding, Karin C. 1991. *Formal Spoken Arabic: Basic Course.* Washington, D.C.: Georgetown University Press.

Schultz, Eckehard, Günther Krahl, and Wolfgang Reuschel. 2000. *Standard Arabic: An Elementary-Intermediate Course.* Cambridge: Cambridge University Press.

Younes, Muther A. 1999. *Intermediate Arabic: An Integrated Approach.* New Haven, Conn.: Yale University Press.

On Arabic Literature

Included here are some recent general works in English that can serve as introductions to various topics in Arabic literature.

Allen, Roger. 1995. *The Arabic Novel: An Historical and Critical Introduction.* Syracuse, N.Y.: Syracuse University Press.

——-. 1998. *The Arabic Literary Heritage: The Development of its Genres and Criticism.* Cambridge: Cambridge University Press.

——-. 2000. *An Introduction to Arabic Literature.* Cambridge: Cambridge University Press.

Zwettler, Michael. 1978. *The Oral Tradition of Classical Arabic Poetry.* Columbus: Ohio State University Press.

Supplementary Bibliography on Colloquial Arabic

Overviews

Brustad, Kristen. 2000. *The Syntax of Spoken Arabic.* Washington, D.C.: Georgetown University Press.

Durand, Olivier. 1995. *Introduzione ai Dialetti Arabi.* Milan: Centro Studi Camito-Semitici.

Holes, Clive. 1995. *Modern Arabic: Structures, Functions, and Varieties.* London: Longman.

Nydell, Margaret. (unpublished; available in draft form) 1994. *Introduction to Colloquial Arabic.* Arlington, Va: Diplomatic Language Services.

Versteegh, Kees. 1997. *The Arabic Language.* New York: Columbia University.

Maghrebi

Ben Amor, Taoufik. 1990. *A Beginner's Course in Tunisian Arabic.* Tunis: Peace Corps.

Inglefield, Ben-Hamza, and Abida. 1970. *Tunisian Arabic Basic Course*, two vols. Bloomington: Indiana University Press.

Owens, Jonathan. 1984. *A Short Reference Grammar of Eastern Libyan Arabic.* Wiesbaden: Harrassowitz.

Tripolitanian Arabic. 1966. Beirut: Foreign Service Institute.

Egyptian/Sudanese

Abdel-Massih, Ernest. 1975. *An Introduction to Egyptian Arabic.* Ann Arbor: University of Michigan Press.

Abdulaziz, Salah. 1985. *Sudanese Arabic Fast Course.* Washington, D.C.: Foreign Service Institute.

Egyptian Arabic and *Egyptian Arabic Fast Course.* 1985. Washington, D.C.: Foreign Service Institute.

El-Tonsi, Abbas. 1992. *Egyptian Colloquial Arabic, A Structure Review*. Cairo: Arabic Language Institute, AUC Press.

Hinds and Bedawi. 1986. *A Dictionary of Egyptian Arabic, Arabic-English*. Beirut: Librairie du Liban.

McGuirk, Russell. 1986. *Colloquial Arabic of Egypt*. (audio tapes included). London: Routledge.

Stevens and Salib. 1987. *A Pocket Dictionary of the Spoken Arabic of Cairo, English-Arabic.* Cairo: AUC Press.

Levantine

Ambros, Arne. 1977. *Damascus Arabic.* Malibu: Undena.

Harb and Nasr. 1973. *An Intermediate Colloquial Arabic Course (Levantine).* Beirut: Librairie du Liban.

Hussein, Lutfi. 1993. *Levantine Arabic for Non-Natives*. New Haven, Conn.: Yale University Press.

McCarus, Qafisheh, and Rammuny. 1978. *A Course in Levantine Arabic.* Ann Arbor: University of Michigan Press.

McLoughlin, Leslie. 1982. *Colloquial Arabic (Levantine).* (with audio tapes.) London: Routledge.

McLoughlin, Leslie. 1979. *A Further Course in Colloquial Arabic (Levantine).* Beirut: Librairie du Liban.

Nasr, Raja. 1989. *Communicate in Colloquial Arabic (Levantine).* Beirut: Librairie du Liban.

Rice and Said. 1979. *Eastern Arabic (Levantine)*. Washington, D.C.: Georgetown University Press.

Peninsular

Holes, Clive. 1990. *Gulf Arabic*. London: Routledge.

——. 1984. *Colloquial Arabic of the Gulf and Saudi Arabia.* London: Routledge. (with tapes)

Ingham, Bruce. 1994. *Najdi Arabic: Central Arabian.* Philadelphia: Benjamins.

——. 1982. *Northeast Arabian dialects*. London: Routledge.

Omar, Margaret. 1975. *Saudi Arabic: Urban Hijazi Dialect.* Washington, D.C.: Foreign Service Institute.

Qafisheh, Hamdi. 1992. *Yemeni Arabic Reference Grammar.* Kensington, MD: Dunwoody Press.

——. 1990. *Yemeni Arabic*. Beirut: Librairie du Liban.

——. 1979. *Gulf Arabic, Intermediate Level*. Tucson: University of Arizona Press.

——. 1977. *A Short Reference Grammar of Gulf Arabic*. Tucson: University of Arizona Press.

——. 1975. *A Basic Course in Gulf Arabic.* Tucson: University of Arizona Press.

Watson, Janet. 1996. *Sbahtu! A Course in San'ani Arabic.* Wiesbaden: Harrassowitz.

——. 1993. *A Syntax of San'ani Arabic*. Wiesbaden: Harrassowitz.